People at Work

The Independent Study Supplement and Teacher's Book

Edgar Sather, Catherine Sadow and George Draper

with photographs by Michael Jerald

PRO LINGUA **ASSOCIATES**

Publishers

Published by Pro Lingua Associates
P.O. Box 1348
Brattleboro, Vermont 05302

802-257-7779
San 216 0579

*At Pro Lingua, our objective is to foster
an approach to learning and teaching which
we call* **Interplay,** *the* **inter***action of language
learners and teachers with their materials,
with the language and the culture, and
with each other in active, creative
and productive* **play.**

People at Work is an adaption of *It's All in a Day's Work* by George Draper and Edgar Sather, which was published and copyrighted © in 1977 by Newbury House Publishers, Inc., of Rowley, Massachusetts, and revised in 1980. The authors and the publisher are grateful to Newbury House for permission to develop and publish this adaptation.

The authors and publisher are also grateful to Douglas William Clegg and to ASCAP for permission to use lyrics and Mr. Clegg's recordings of the three songs used in Lesson 5: *Fill My Thirst, California,* and *You Get What's Coming.* Copyright © 1988 by Douglas William Clegg. All rights reserved.

To purchase Mr. Clegg's recordings or to arrange for personal appearances, write D. W. Clegg, 328 Concord Stage Road, Weare, New Hampshire 03281, or call 603-529-1051.

The publisher acknowledges the tireless and creative services of Edgar Sather as both interviewer and impresario, contributions to this book far beyond the call to duty as author. Thank you.

ISBN 0-86647-036-0

This independent study supplement/teacher's book is designed to be used with a student's book and three tapes.

People at Work was set in Electra by Stevens Graphics of Brattleboro, Vermont, and printed and bound by Capital City Press of Montpelier, Vermont. It was designed by Arthur A. Burrows.

Printed in the United States of America. Fourth printing 2012

Acknowledgements

Many people generously contributed their time, advice, skills, talents in the preparation of this book. We herewith acknowledge our indebtedness and our gratitude for their valuable assistance:

◆ First of all to those who served as *primae dramatis personae:* Patrick Doherty, Beatrice Cespedes de Fantini, Matt Skeele, Robin Fitzgerald, Douglas Clegg, Jane Grube, Robert Peoples, Rupa Cousins, Brooks Brown, Connie Snow; and Neal Wach, Sophie Draper, and Sam Avram.

◆ And the *secundae dramatis personnae:* Dyer Drake, Javier Castro-Wan, Annie Quest, Elise Burrows, Karen Peoples, David Woodbury, Naima Rodriguez, Ingrid Burrows, Alia Thurrell, Robert Jordan, Budi Wanati, James Zarndt, Tala Halabi, Carol Ochs, Al Stockwell, Paul Sather, and Janice Rucker Sather.

◆ And the *terciae dramatis personae:* Fritz Hewitt, Tony Potter, Steve Patch, Susanne Ramsey, Dick Ramsey, Susan Spanger, Ruth Rousseau, Richard Rousseau, Mike Spurrier, Russell Nadeau, Jill Eyre, Tim Hayes, Randy Knaggs, and Cami Elliott-Knaggs.

◆ To those who facilitated production operations: Barbara Gentry for the Brattleboro Memorial Hospital, Larry Alpert at the Academy School, Robert Neubauer at the Walnut Street School, Ruth Rousseau at the Bank of Vermont, Susanna Ramsey at Casa del Sol, and Jonathan Szarvas of the Fifth Season Restaurant.

◆ To Douglas Clegg, who graciously consented to our including three of the songs from his record album, "Fill My Thirst."

◆ To Michael Gray, who granted us the use of two of his piano pieces from his album, "Invocation," as background in the Neal Wade interview and the lunch-at-the-restaurant section.

◆ To Al Stockwell, who painstakingly and masterfully supervised the production and editing of the tapes.

◆ To Mike Jerald, who creatively snapped the photos.

◆ To the students and teachers of the English Language Center at Northeastern University in Boston who worked with the materials and gave valuable suggestions.

At our insistence, we, the authors, wish to give our deepest salaams to publisher and editor Andy Burrows, who initiated and encouraged the project and also shared unstintingly of his advice and creative energy. His name should appear as a co-author.

Cathy thanks the three J's in her life — Joshua, Jonathan, and Jerome, who patiently taped, read, and listened during the formative stages of the book; Edgar thanks Geoffrey and Paul who found their ways of encouraging the project; George thanks the whole world in general, with special mentions of Charlotte, Whitney, and Jeanette.

And now, before we outdo the Academy Awards presenters, we hope you'll get acquainted with our *People at Work.*

Lesson format

A. Prelistening

Note to the teacher or tutor*

Introductory reading

Work related vocabulary list with definitions*

B. The First Listening

The Interview — *on tape* — tape script*

Questions after the interview, first listening

Vocabulary in context exercise — *on tape*
— tape script* and definitions*

C. The Second Listening

The Interview again — *on tape*

Questions after the interview, second listening*

Reconstruction exercise

D. The Dialogue

The Dialogue — *on tape* — tape script*

Questions after the dialogue

Interactive listening exercise — *on tape*
— tapescript* and answers*

E. Communicative Activities

The Projects, instructions, forms, and readings

Materials in this book are marked with an asterisk

Contents

Suggestions
for the student working
independently

This book is called a supplement. If you are studying independently without a teacher or a class, you will need it, but your student's book and your tapes are the most important parts of these materials. In this introduction, we will give you some suggestions on how to use the materials and how to study English on your own.

You may have several reasons for working with *People at Work* independently. You may not have a native speaking teacher or tutor, you may not have a class to work with, or you may not have native speakers of English who can conveniently take time to work with you. You may not have a time when you can schedule an English course, or you may be studying overseas where it is difficult to find opportunities to use English actively. In writing *People at Work*, our first concern has been to develop your listening skills, the more passive side of communication. If listening is your most important concern, you will find the interviews, dialogues, and listening exercises both interesting and challenging. The people whom we recorded are all native speakers (with two exceptions), and they all speak quickly, naturally, and idiomatically. If you use the tapes and do the exercises and do nothing else, you will strengthen your listening skills.

However, *People at Work* also gives you the chance to build the more active communicative skills as well — not only speaking and pronunciation but also the skills you need for conversation and serious discussion. To build these skills, you will have to find English speakers and/or other English students to communicate with. For many of the exercises, we recommend that you work with a partner or in a small discussion group. If possible, even if you don't have a tutor, you should find one or more students to share your studies with. This not only makes your work more interesting, but it also lets you use your listening skills as part of real communication; you listen to the tape and then apply what you learn actively and naturally in conversation.

In order to build your listening skills quickly, **it is very important that you listen to each of the taped sections before reading the scripts that are given in this book.** Of course, it is tempting to read first. It is much easier to read before you listen. It is also much easier to look over the comprehension questions in this book in which the questions and scripts are given. Use your student's book with your tape. Keep this book closed. Don't give in to temptation. Learn to depend on your ears and not just your eyes. If you don't, English will never be a living language for you. This is the basic rule to follow: **use your student's book and the tape first!**

The communicative activities or projects suggested at the end of each lesson in your student's book are the second stage in teaching you to listen and then to communicate in English. They are specifically designed to put you in situations in which you will find it natural to speak English and to use it in practical ways to obtain information. With these projects, we intend to get you out of your room, away from your tape recorder, and into the English speaking community where you can learn to use your English — and incidentally get to know people with whom you can use it. If you are not studying in an English speaking country, this is more difficult to do, but the projects can be adapted.

The projects in *People at Work* ask you to gather information either about aspects of the work being discussed or of American culture. In many lessons, a short article is given in your student's book and you are asked to read it as part of one of the projects. In most projects, you are asked to get specific information from English speakers in your school or the community. In all of the projects, you are asked to make a verbal or written presentation in your class on the research or reading you have done. Even if you are overseas, you can always do the project which requires a reading and then write out your "presentation." However, no matter where you are, you can adapt other projects as well; it will just take some imagination. For example, in the lesson about the small business owner, you can find people who run their own businesses, interview them in your own language if they don't speak English, and then write about your findings in English or explain them to an English speaking friend, comparing what you learned in *People at Work* with what you learned from your interview and discussing any questions your friend may have.

In summary, if you are using *People at Work* independently without a teacher or a class, 1) whenever possible, do the exercises with one or more English speaking fellow students, 2) always listen first before you look at the scripts or questions in this book, and 3) adapt the projects to your situation using as much English as you can.

Studying a language on your own takes a lot of self-discipline, imagination, creativity, and hard work. We hope you will find lots of interesting material in our book both to work with and to share so that your learning will also be fun. Good luck.

Suggestions for the teacher

In using all of *People at Work*, you will be helping your students work on two types of communicative skills, the more passive or receptive listening skills and the whole constellation of active communicative skills needed for social interaction, group planning, classroom presentations, and purposeful discussion. However, it is certainly not necessary to use all of this book. Depending on the particular class at hand, you will undoubtedly use the book in different ways. You may wish to use it to study specific occupations with their related vocabulary or specific social or personal issues which may be relevant to your students lives and understanding of the culture. You may wish to work primarily on listening skills and thus use only the tapes and listening exercises accompanying them. Or you may wish to work primarily on the projects, using the taped material only as an introduction to these communicative activities. So that you can take full advantage of these materials in your own way, we have included in this introduction an explanation of the intent and structure of *People at Work* and some suggestions on how to use it to the best advantage.

Our intent

When we began to write this book, we hoped to provide students with an affordable book and several hours of tapes which would be both interesting and insightful about the work Americans do. We were also interested, as indicated above, in finding ways of working on the whole communicative process, in getting students out of the classroom and into the community to use the language they are learning. In developing the book, we also added some readings relevant to the jobs the people do, listening activities which help the students practice useful skills like note taking, and discussion topics chosen to develop their understanding of our North American attitudes about work and of a host of other cultural issues.

The audience

Who should use the book and at what proficiency level? It has been field tested in both intermediate and advanced pre-university intensive English programs as well as in one intensive program for new immigrants at an upper intermediate level. Although the vocabulary is sophisticated and the language informal and idiomatic, the pace of all the listenings is natural and leisurely. Both intermediate and advanced students have found the materials interesting and challenging.

The book can be used in business training and orientation programs, in adult education courses, and with older high school students who are beginning to think about jobs after graduation or about going on for more education. In short, *People at Work* can be used with any students at the intermediate to advanced level who would find these people and their work relevant.

One aspect which we feel particularly recommends our book to you if you are working with students who are considering entering the Canadian or U.S. work force is that each person interviewed for *People at Work* is in some real sense a role model, enjoying his or her life and successful at what he or she has chosen to do. Each is a complex person with weaknesses and problems as well as virtues to be emulated, and to the extent that we have captured this complexity and ambiguity, we believe we have brought our book to life.

Can a book focused so clearly on communicative skills be used successfully for independent study either in North America or overseas? We feel that it can if the students and their teacher or tutor understand the problems inherent in self-study and how to use this book, the supplement and teacher's book. If your students are planning to do independent study, we recommend that they read all three introductions in this book thoughtfully, bearing in mind the following two points.

First, if your students are only interested in building their listening skills, this book can be used easily and anywhere for independent study. The trick is to teach your students to go beyond the listening and to use their environment effectively. In an English speaking community, the possibilities are legion. Overseas, the opportunities for using English are naturally limited, but the projects will prove to be challenging vehicles for growth for those who are resourceful.

Second, a student doing independent study should have the entire learning package, including not only the student's book and the tapes but also much of the material in this book: the tape scripts, the definitions of the vocabulary, and the "Suggestions for the student working independently."

Structure and use of these materials

Although the lessons in *People at Work* vary slightly in format, they generally follow the same plan. Each element of the lessons is explained below, but here, for easy reference, is a complete outline in chart form listing the elements. The elements can be used selectively and you can vary the order, but we recommend the order in which they are listed. As you see from the chart, some of the elements appear only in the student's book, others only in the teacher's book.

The placement of the projects may seem confusing at first. Although they appear at the end of each lesson in the student's book, they are shown here following the prelistening material. This is to indicate that we recommend that they be introduced early in teaching each lesson and then done concurrently with the listening elements. We often end each lesson with the students' presentations on their projects.

Lesson Element	Tape	Student's book	Teacher's book
Introductory note to the teacher or tutor			X
PRELISTENING			
The Introductory Reading 🕮		X	
Work Related Vocabulary, word list only		X	
word list with definitions			X
THE COMMUNICATIVE ACTIVITIES			
The Projects: choices, instructions,			
forms, readings, etc. 🖎		X	
THE FIRST LISTENING			
The Interview, first listening ✳	X		
tape script			X
Questions after the interview		X	
Vocabulary in Context exercise, listening ✳	X		
worksheet to be filled out		X	
tape script and idiom definitions			X
THE SECOND LISTENING			
The Interview again, second listening ✳	X		
Questions, detailed comprehension			X
Portrait photograph for discussion		X	
Reconstruction exercise		X	
THE DIALOGUE			
The Dialogue, listening ✳	X		
tape script			X
Action photograph for discussion		X	
Questions after the dialogue		X	
Interactive Listening exercise, listening ✳	X		
worksheet to be filled out		X	
tape script and answers			X

The Introductory Reading 🕮

Each chapter begins with an introductory reading which introduces the person and explains a little bit about his or her career. These introductions can be read in the classroom or at home and then discussed as a prelistening exercise.

Work Related Vocabulary

The introductory reading is followed by another pre-listening exercise, a list of work related vocabulary which comes up in the taped interview. Although the story can generally be understood even if the student does not know or remember all of this vocabulary, the section is meant to be used in class before the students begin listening to the tape. The definitions of these words are included in the teacher's book and deliberately omitted from the student's book. In addition to the work related vocabulary, a few other words and expressions from the interview are often listed for the students to review before listening to the interview.

Our recommended way to have the students deal with the meanings of these words is to have them work together in small discussion groups. If the student knows a particular word, he or she can check it off and share the meaning with the group. If no student knows a particular vocabulary item, one of them can look it up in a dictionary and share the meaning with the others. The students can write the word in their native language or a meaning for it in English in the space provided in their books. And, of course, you as the teacher are always there as a source of information and insight. In this way, vocabulary gets discussed and recycled and will probably be better remembered than it would be if the definitions were provided. This procedure also gives students an occasion for purposeful discussion — always a desirable activity in the classroom.

The Projects

Although the projects are presented at the end of each lesson in the student's book, we recommend that they be done concurrently with the listening work. We usually introduce them in class after we have discussed the work related vocabulary. Depending on its complexity, a project generally will take from one to four or five hours for a student to prepare. Some projects take some students much more time.

The students can group together as they read over the projects and then decide who will do which project and whether he or she will work alone or with one or more classmates. The students can then discuss how they will proceed, and they can make arrangements at this time to get together outside of class to plan further and to carry out the project.

If the students are in an English-speaking community, the projects should, of course, be conducted in English. If the students are in a country where the native language is not English, they can do the planning in English, the research in their native language, and the oral presentation in English.

Although some students may not have time to do some of the projects (for example, they may be working all day and thus not able to get information from offices which are open only from nine to five), there are many projects which can be done at home. In fact, you may find that some of the projects will seem so useful to some of your students (for example, banking or health projects for new immigrants) that they will want to find a way to do them. You may also be inspired to come up with variations on some of the projects which will particularly fit your students' needs and schedules.

The main goals of the projects are to give students the opportunity 1) to interact with each other through planning and working together, 2) to use English out in the community, 3) to discover useful information, and 4) the opportunity to organize and present material to a group. For students who are shy about approaching outsiders, there are some projects which do not require a lot of community interaction. These students may feel more comfortable if they are paired up with more outgoing students.

The Interview

This is the longest of the four listening sections. The students will probably listen to it at least twice. Before the first listening, the students have been given some orientation through the introductory reading and some vocabulary which comes up in the interview. *They should not be given a tape script.* The questions which are given in their student's book have been carefully written to give no clues about what to listen for. We hope that, in both the first and second listenings, the students will depend on their ears and not their eyes and memories.

In each of the ten interviews, the same interviewer talks to a person about his or her work.

6

He generally asks what the person's job consists of, how he or she got into it, and what the advantages and disadvantages of the job are. In the process, he discovers quite a lot about the individual's personality and personal concerns.

The first listening is followed in the student's book by a few, very general comprehension questions. In order to answer them, the students need to get only the general gist of the interview. The first listening can be done at home, in a language lab, or in class, depending on your preference and your students'. However, it is very effective in the classroom where group discussion, possibly based on the questions, can follow immediately. The questions can also be answered in writing.

Vocabulary in Context

From each of the interviews, we have chosen five or six idioms. The exercise using them has three objectives. One is simply to give the students practice in listening attentively and thoughtfully. A second is to give them practice in guessing the meanings of strange idioms from context. The third is to recycle sections of the interview after the first listening, which should make the second, closer listening easier. This exercise is suitable for listening homework. In a few lessons, additional idioms are given in the teacher's book, and you can present these in class.

The Interview — second listening ✵

After they have answered the first set of comprehension questions and done the vocabulary in context exercise, the students should rewind their tapes and listen to the interview a second time. In this teacher's book, there are more detailed comprehension questions to be asked at this time. You can ask them orally, or you can photocopy them and hand them out as a stimulus to group or written work. They are not given in the student's book because many students would read them first and then listen for the answers — a valid but less profitable procedure.

The Reconstruction exercise

A list of key phrases from the interview is given in the student's book. In explaining how these phrases were used, the students reconstruct the dialogue, often shifting the narrative into the third person and the past. Students can work in small groups. For example, one student might read the phrase: "Especially the janitor!" (This is from Lesson 2: Dolores Silva.) Her classmate might respond with a reconstruction something like this: "Especially the janitor. Oh, I remember. Dolores said this when the interviewer asked her what kinds of jobs she did, and she said she was the secretary and the bookkeeper. When he asked, "Are you also the janitor?" she said, "Yes, especially the janitor!!!" The students proceed from phrase to phrase in this manner until they have reconstructed much of the interview. This exercise is also useful for recycling the vocabulary.

The photographs

In each lesson, there are two photographs, a portrait of the person featured and a picture of his or her work place. They are decorative, of course, but they can also be used as a basis for discussion after the students have listened to the interview. The students will practice their new vocabulary as they talk about their personal and cross-cultural reactions to the person and his or her work. In Lesson 10, for example, does Connie Snow look like a building contractor or not, and why?

7

The Dialogue ✳

The dialogues are short. Generally, they elaborate on a situation referred to or a comment made in the interview. They also develop some of the cultural and personal issues which we have found to be of greatest interest to our students. Questions follow each dialogue. We have not made any attempt to point out or define the vocabulary and idioms in the dialogues since there is already so much vocabulary development in each lesson, but we recognize that this is a rich resource for you if your students are willing and able.

Interactive Listening ✳

Although the activities in this section vary, they are always task oriented. The student is asked to listen to the taped material and then, based on what he or she hears, to do some task such as filling out a medical form or finding the error in a checkbook or making out checks for four people in a restaurant. In some cases the answers are given in this teacher's book, but in some cases the students are asked to make a free choice (as when they match up volunteers with volunteer jobs in Lesson 6) and in other cases their answers may be personal and open-ended (as in Lesson 4 on Bertha Haynes). Because students often have to listen to this section several times, it is a very appropriate one for homework either at home or in the language lab. It can then serve as a vehicle for classroom discussion.

A word about photocopying: Since every student should have his or her own copy of the student's book and the tapes, there is no reason to copy these and permission to do so is not granted. On the other hand, it may be helpful to give students copies of some of the materials in this teacher's book and so you are encouraged to copy the following: 1) any of the definitions of the work related vocabulary and vocabulary in context, 2) the comprehension questions to be asked after the second listening to each interview, 3) the transcriptions of the interviews and the dialogues, and 4) the tape scripts and answers to the vocabulary in context and interactive listening exercises. Again, you may copy the material from this book which is listed above. Permission is not granted to copy the student's book or the tapes.

A word about using the student's book as a workbook: We recommend it. If you can possibly afford to supply a book to each student or if you can have your students buy themselves books, they will discover that writing in the book and recording their vocabulary, reactions, and answers to questions in the workbook next to the pictures and readings will help them get and stay involved with the materials. Furthermore, seeing their own notes, errors, and successes written in their books, will remind them vividly of the work they have done and all the vocabulary and cultural insights they have gained. It is a very effective way of encouraging students to review. An additional advantage to having the students have their own workbooks and tapes is that they can continue working on their own after your course is finished.

We hope that your students and you enjoy *People at Work* and that you find the books and tapes interesting, productive, and easy to use in the classroom.

Suggestions for the tutor

Whether or not you are a trained teacher, whether or not you are a native speaker, the curriculum built into *People at Work* will be effective in helping your students to understand natural, idiomatic English when it is spoken to them and in getting them to speak; it will give them practice, of course, but also the confidence they need to go out and use their English. If they are in an English speaking community, *People at Work* will also help them understand the culture around them and give them some positive role models from the working world.

Many tutors have not been trained as teachers or, more specifically, have not been trained to teach English as a language. If you are one of these, here are some points to consider:

If your students are living in an English-speaking community, they can pick up much of the English they need from their environment. You need not provide them with a full course of studies covering all skills, but as a tutor, you can respond to their special needs and you can help them use their environment in learning English — *People at Work* is designed to help in this. And, as a tutor, you have many other roles to play.

You are a friend and confidant with whom the personal strains of cross-cultural adjustment can be discussed. Many of the issues focused on in the listenings and projects in *People at Work* will bring your student's concerns out naturally so that you can share them and help.

You are a prime resource for information about the language and the culture. You need not have all the answers. You do need to show your student how to explore his or her questions, and you need to share that exploration process. Another way of saying this is that, as a tutor, it is more important to teach your students how to learn English and how to learn about the culture around them than to teach them specific information. What you need is a vehicle for your explorations — something specific to talk about — and you will find lots of vehicles in both the listenings and the projects of this book.

Your students need to practice their skills. As tutor, you are the most available and safest person they can practice on. If they can make you understand, other people can understand too. Throughout *People at Work*, the students are asked to work in pairs or in small groups and to make presentations in English and then to discuss the issues involved. If you are working one-on-one with a student, you are it; you have to carry half of all the discussion. Preferably, you will be able to get a small group together so that the students can share their struggles, discoveries, and triumphs with peers. You can then participate — and you should — but you can also maintain some distance from the discussion allowing you to make objective observations.

9

There are many ways to bring grammar into a tutorial study. It need not, and usually should not, be a prime focus. While working on *People at Work*, your students will do a lot of speaking and writing, and you will notice mistakes they are making (among your objective observations). If you use a simple unsequenced grammar, you can use it to explain the mistakes they are making and let them practice the structures they need. *The Grammar Handbook* by Nancy Clair, published by Pro Lingua, is easy to use this way.

Many of the suggestions given in this book for the teacher and for the student working independently will be helpful to you as a tutor. They explain the structure and use of *People at Work*, but more importantly they suggest the underlying principle which should guide you as a tutor. You should expect your students to work together, to help each other, and to use their environment in many different ways to practice their English and explore the culture. Let them use you, but put the burden of understanding, of learning, on them. You cannot learn English for them. You can only teach them how to learn. As Dr. Maria Montessori said, "Help me to help myself."

If you are a tutor working in a non-English-speaking community, most of what we have said above applies to your situation. The difference is in stress. Since it is difficult to find ways of getting your students out to speak to native speakers, 1) when the occasion arises, be sure to make the most of it (the projects will help), and 2) you and fellow students in the tutorial group must provide most of the practice with and insights into the language. Because of this, it is particularly important that you establish an open, sharing relationship with your students. If you honestly respect and value them in the their roles, they will not respect you less if you lower the traditional teacher/student barriers and really communicate with them. You have nothing to lose and everything to gain because the ability to communicate in English across your cultural barriers is the goal you and your students are working toward.

And lastly, you will probably find some of these people at work amusing and so will your students. Share your reactions, and enjoy the book.

Lesson One

Freddy Gallagher

Bank Teller

Note to the teacher or tutor:

This first lesson is a typical one in format with its initial interview and follow-up dialogue, its two taped vocabulary exercises, the reconstruction exercise, and three sets of questions — the first two about the interview, very general questions followed by the detailed comprehension questions given only in this book, and a third set of discussion questions following the dialogue. And then there are the communicative activities or projects suggested in the student's book. This typical format will be followed throughout with some variations.

However, Freddy is not typical. At any rate he is not what most people from other cultures think of as a typical North American. He likes his work, but he doesn't want to "get ahead." He enjoys his job and the life it lets him lead. Who is to say he isn't successful? Actually, of course, he isn't really atypical at all. There are lots of people who are happy where they are, doing what they are doing. This may lead your students to an interesting discussion of their cultural stereotypes and expectations.

There are seven projects to choose from in the first lesson, three of which involve interviews. In the student's book as part of the second lesson, there are some suggestions on how to prepare for and handle interviews. These suggestions are not given in the first lesson for three reasons: 1) they will mean more to the students after they have done an interview, 2) the projects in the second lesson are all interviews and somewhat more challenging, and 3) with seven projects to choose from, lesson one gives the students enough to read without introducing an additional element. However, you may want to read over the suggestions yourself before introducing the idea of projects to your class.

A specific note *on the reading in Project Seven at the end of this lesson (pages 9–11 in the student's book): the text comes from a brochure based primarily on oral English. It is compiled from the transcription of an interview and informal notes. Since it is sometimes ungrammatical and unstructured, you may want to point out to your students that it is not meant to be a model for formal writing.*

Introductory Reading ✍

This reading, which is given in the student's book on page 1, should be discussed as a pre-listening exercise.

11

Work Related Vocabulary — with definitions

1. a **bank teller**: a bank employee who has contact with customers and primarily takes care of their deposits and withdrawals

2. a **time card**: a card that records an employee's arrival and departure time each day

3. a **vault**: a room or compartment often made of steel for the safekeeping of valuables. It is sometimes called a "safe."

4. **cash and change**: ready money; currency; coins

5. a **deposit slip**: a piece of paper filled out by the customer indicating how much money is to be put into the account

6. a **withdrawal slip**: a piece of paper filled out by the customer indicating how much money is to be taken out of the account

7. **credit and debit slips**: pieces of paper given to a customer after a transaction is complete indicating that money has been put into (credited to) or taken out of (debited from) an account

8. **paper clips**: bent pieces of wire used to hold two or more pieces of paper together

9. a **rubber stamp**: This is a piece of rubber with a design or writing raised on its surface. It is usually attached to a handle. When stamped on an ink pad, it then can print ink impressions (of names, dates and the like) on a piece of paper.

10. an **ink pad**: a piece of soft substance held in a small container and saturated with ink. A rubber stamp is pressed on it before the stamp is pressed on to paper.

11. **to sign on**: to make contact with the computer

12. a **station**: the special place or position where a teller works

13. a **teller number**: Each teller has a number that gives him access to the computer. He will be responsible for what is entered under his number.

14. a **secret code number**: Not everyone can get information that is very private from the computer. The computer will only give it to people who know a special combination of numbers or letters.

15. **to access**: to make contact with the computer

16. **to punch in**: to press the computer keys to enter the customer's account number

17. an **account number**: Every customer at the bank has a number which represents his or her business with the bank.

18. **transactions**: Everything that is done by the customer is a transaction. If you take money out of your account, that is a transaction. If you put money into your account, that is another transaction. If you move money from one account into another account, that is another transaction.

19. **"the computer is down"**: The computer is not working.

20. **pass books**: Very often, people with savings accounts have a small account book which they must use when they go to the bank. All of their transactions are recorded in it.

21. **loans**: If you need money and don't have it, the bank will consider giving it to you. You will return it to them and pay them a certain extra percentage called "interest" as payment for using their money.

22. **money orders**: You can send money by buying a money order and mailing it. Only the person whose name is on the money order can use it.

23. **interest rates**: The percentage you pay when you borrow money is the interest rate. If, for example, you borrow $1000 for a year at a flat annual interest rate of 10%, you must repay $1100.

Additional vocabulary

This vocabulary does not appear on the tape. The teacher can read it to the class.

1. **repetitive**: the same thing over and over again
2. an **ESL book**: an English as a Second Language book
3. **automatic**: involuntary; lacking conscious planning
4. **to revolutionize**: to bring about a radical change

The Interview ✺ 1

Tape: Part One — The first listening

Lesson One of People at Work begins with an interview with bank teller, Freddy Gallagher. Before listening to the interview, review the work related vocabulary in your book. You will listen to the interview at least twice. After the first listening, answer the questions in your student's book on page 3, and then do the vocabulary in context exercise, using both your book and this tape. When you have finished the vocabulary in context, rewind the tape and listen to the interview with Freddy again.

The interview takes place in a small conference room in the bank where Freddy works as a teller. It is twelve o'clock noon, and Freddy is giving part of his lunch break for this interview. Now, Freddy Gallagher, bank teller:

INTERVIEWER. Freddy, it was really very good of you to take your lunch hour for this interview ... thanks a lot.

FREDDY. Hey, the pleasure is mine. It's nice to have someone interested.

INTERVIEWER. Well, one thing I want to ask right off ... I might as well be up front about it. I notice that most of the tellers in the bank, actually, most of the tellers in town, I've noticed, are women. It's kind of a women's world, bank telling, it seems. What I want to know is if it's difficult being a man in this woman's world?

FREDDY. Well. I'm not quite sure how to answer that. Hm. I guess it is at times, you know, as far as, I don't know, trying to be involved in their conversations during free times or break times, you know, like when they're talking about shopping for this or that, or talking about their boy friends or women's problems in general, I feel like I stick out like a sore thumb. It's embarrassing sometimes. But other than that, it's no big deal actually.

INTERVIEWER. So, no big difficulty, then.

FREDDY. Not really, except for all the people that ask me about it.

INTERVIEWER. Ooops! Sorry about that. But now, about your real work here. What do you do here, actually? Could you just give me a little idea about your work.

FREDDY. Sure. I'm a bank teller here at the bank. Basically, to be honest, my work is quite repetitive and not very exciting ....same things hour after hour, day after day. Most people hate that kind of work, but I really like it. You see, I'm sort of a dreamer.

INTERVIEWER. A dreamer? In a bank?

FREDDY. It's true. I love to daydream, and a bank teller can daydream.

INTERVIEWER. Oh now, come on. With all that money flowing through your fingers all the time, daydream? Oh, you can't be serious!

FREDDY. Now, don't misunderstand. My job isn't always that easy.

INTERVIEWER. Well, I wouldn't think so.

FREDDY. But the way I look at it, it requires less concentration than other jobs, but on the other hand, it does require more organization, which is different from concentration, if you get what I mean.

INTERVIEWER. Eh, well, maybe I will if you give me more of an idea of just what do you do ... a typical day, that sort of thing.

FREDDY. Typical day. O.K. Let's see ... here's a typical day in the life of Freddy Gallagher — just what you want for your ESL book, right?

INTERVIEWER. Exactly.

FREDDY. First of all, when the bank opens at nine o'clock every morning, I have to be completely ready for work. So I usually get there about 8:00, 8:15, fill in my time card and start to get ready. I go to my special section in the big vault and get the cash and change I need and put the cash in my drawer. Then I check my materials. I get my deposit slips, my withdrawal slips, credit and debit slips —enough for the whole day — and arrange them in my drawer. Then I check to be sure that I've got everything I need within reach: pencils, pens, paper clips, rubber stamp, ink pad. All that's got to be done before I open my station at nine o'clock.

13

INTERVIEWER. Oh, our students are going to love this, Freddy. It's so nice and neat and typical. But go on, we breathlessly await what happens next?

FREDDY. You're pulling my leg?

INTERVIEWER. Now Freddy, are you pulling mine?

FREDDY. Huh? Come on, no more leg pulling. OK? Now, where was I? Oh yes. The last thing I do before facing the gathering mob scene, I make sure the computer is working. It is, and then I sign on and enter my teller number and my secret code number which accesses me to the computer.

INTERVIEWER. The computer really has revolutionized banking, hasn't it.

FREDDY. Oh, it's great. I punch in the customer's account number and I get a history of his or her account, all the transactions on that account for a certain period of time.

INTERVIEWER. .... all the deposits, withdrawals, debits, credits.

FREDDY. Yeah, that's it. It's great, except for the times when the computer is down. Then there are real headaches. Anyway, I've got myself prepared and open up my station at 9, I'm ready for work ... and ready for daydreaming.

INTERVIEWER. Well, you do insist on that daydreaming, don't you.

FREDDY. You've got it.

INTERVIEWER. But, in between the daydreamings, you "work"?

FREDDY. Well, that's what they call it. Sure. People come and go. Most of them deposit checks or withdraw money from their checking accounts or savings accounts. Sometimes they do both. Then occasionally, customers require special help from me. For example, they may lose their pass books, and I have to make new ones. Or maybe they want to write money orders or ask about loans, things like that.

INTERVIEWER. Well, are you trained to answer questions about loans?

FREDDY. No. Not really. ... I'm not a loan officer, but I can answer simple questions about interest rates or the bank's loan policies. If I can't answer them, I send them on to one of the loan officers. And to tell the truth, at those times, I have to stop daydreaming and concentrate.

INTERVIEWER. So you're saying that most of that other stuff is really quite easy, almost automatic.

FREDDY. Right. That's the word, automatic. Sure, there are other jobs harder than mine. Certainly. There are other jobs with higher pay and greater responsibility. I know a lot of people who are richer than I am. Who needs it? I don't. I don't know many guys who are happier. Strange as it may sound, I don't know many who are freer.

INTERVIEWER. Freer?

FREDDY. Yeah, freer. Now, most people don't understand this.

INTERVIEWER. Huh, well, but do you really like this job of yours.

FREDDY. Sure I do ... I'm not crazy. Like I said, I'm a dreamer.

INTERVIEWER. O.K. What do you daydream about?

FREDDY. What do I daydream about?

INTERVIEWER. Yeah.

FREDDY. Everything. I often daydream about my life outside the bank. I daydream about my vacations. My weekends. My nights. Especially my nights. Most people dream at night and live during the day. But I dream during the day and live at night.

INTERVIEWER. Would you explain that maybe a little more clearly.

FREDDY. No way. I can't. I'm a bank teller, not a poet.

Vocabulary in Context ✳ 2

Tape: Part Two — Listening exercise

Listen to this recording and write down the word or phrase you hear. You will hear the word or phrase twice. Then, listen to two sentences in which that word or phrase is used. The second sentence is taken from the conversation you've just heard. Next, on page 3, write down what you think that word or phrase means. Make an intelligent guess, using context clues.

1. **Up front**   up front
   Example: You aren't telling me what you really think! Please be up front with me.
   From the tape: One thing I want to ask right off. I might as well be up front about it.

2. **To stick out like a sore thumb**   to stick out like a sore thumb
   Example: Everyone else who goes to the dance school dances beautifully, but I have two left feet and when I dance I stick out like a sore thumb.
   From the tape: I feel like I stick out like a sore thumb.

3. **No big deal**   no big deal
   Example: You're going to be a little late for my party? No big deal. When can you come?
   From the tape: It's embarrassing sometimes, but other than that it's no big deal.

4. **To pull one's leg**   to pull one's leg
   Example: When he tells me he's been married fourteen times, he's pulling my leg, right?
   From the tape: FREDDY. You pulling my leg?   INTERVIEWER. Freddy, are you pulling mine?

5. **A mob scene**   a mob scene
   Example: If you want to see a mob scene, go to Times Square in New York City on New Year's Eve. Everybody's there and they're pushing and yelling and screaming.
   From the tape: Last thing I do before facing the gathering mob scene, I make sure the computer is working.

6. **You've got it.**   You've got it.
   Example: Yes, that's exactly what I mean! You've got it!
   From the tape: You've got it!

Additional vocabulary

The following vocabulary is not given on the tape of this exercise. The teacher can read it to the class in the style of the tape script.

7. **Right off**   right off
   Example: Jack knew right off that this was the girl of his dreams. It was love at first sight.
   From the tape: Well, one thing I want to ask right off . . . I might as well be up front about it.

8. **Real headaches**   real headaches
   Example: Mary snarled at her little brothers: "You guys are real headaches! You're making so much noise I can't even think to do my homework!"
   From the tape: It's great, except for the times when the computer is down. Then there are real headaches.

9. **Come and go**   come and go
   Example: I'm feeling fine, doctor, except for the dizzy spells, and they don't bother me all the time. They just come and go.
   From the tape: People come and go. Most of them deposit checks or withdraw money from their checking accounts or savings accounts.

15

Definitions of vocabulary in context

1. direct; honest
2. to be very noticeable because you are very different from everything around you
3. not so important
4. to tease
5. a crowd; a riot
6. At last, you understand completely.
7. right away; immediately
8. annoying problems
9. occur or pass by occasionally

The Interview 1

Tape: Part One, again — The second listening

Rewind the tape and listen to the interview again. Then answer the following questions and do the reconstruction exercise.

Detailed Questions

These detailed comprehension questions may be asked after the second listening to the interview. They do not appear in the student's book.

1. What do we learn about women working in this bank?
2. Freddy goes into detail about his typical day. What do you remember about it?
3. What special help does Freddy sometimes give customers?
4. What does he say about daydreaming?
5. What is his attitude toward his job? Why?
6. Can you explain the "leg pulling?" Who says it to whom? What are they talking about?
7. Do you think that Freddy is good at his work? Why or why not?
8. Would Freddy's work be interesting to you? Why or why not?
9. What do you learn about the interviewer: his interviewing style, his interests, his attitudes, his background?

Reconstruction

The exercise which is given in the student's book on page 4 should be done after the second listening to the interview.

The Dialogue ✳ 3

Tapes: Part Three — A conversation between Freddy and Mr. Holtz

Listen to the dialogue and then answer the questions in your book.

MR. HOLTZ. Freddy, could you step into my office for a minute?

FREDDY. Sure. Right away, sir.

MR. HOLTZ. Good. Sit down, sit down.

FREDDY. Thank you.

MR. HOLTZ. Freddy, uh, I've been wondering . . . Are you happy with your job here?

FREDDY. Oh, yes, sir. I enjoy my work very much.

MR. HOLTZ. But it's not very interesting, is it?

FREDDY. Interesting? Well. . . .

MR. HOLTZ. I mean, you do the same thing every day! Receive cash and deposit it, withdraw cash and pay it out. You know?

FREDDY. Well, that's true. It's not very exciting. But . . . it's pleasant. I like it.

MR. HOLTZ. But, don't you want to advance?

FREDDY. Advance?

MR. HOLTZ. Sure, have a better job! A higher position. Like, how about a job as a loan officer?

FREDDY. A loan officer? Gee, I don't know much about loans, Mr. Holtz.

MR. HOLTZ. Oh, it's easy to learn. I myself started as a loan officer. You could become a vice-president, too.

FREDDY. Well, that's . . . I don't know if . . . .

MR. HOLTZ. Look, I'm only talking about small personal loans. For instance, a customer comes to you. He needs a small amount of money, right?

FREDDY. Well, how much is a small amount?

MR. HOLTZ. Oh, two hundred, five hundred—no more than a thousand. Let's say he wants to buy a TV set, for instance.

FREDDY. All right. And I give him the money?

MR. HOLTZ. Well, of course you have to decide. You ask a few questions. How much money does he earn? Is he paying back other loans? Does he own his own home? That kind of thing.

FREDDY. I see. And then I make a decision about the loan.

MR. HOLTZ. That's right. And you have to be careful. I mean, you really have to concentrate on the details. Well, look, what about it? Are you interested in the job?

FREDDY. It requires concentration, huh?

MR. HOLTZ. Oh, yes, a lot of that. You'll be a tired man at night.

FREDDY. Tired? At night? Oh no, Mr. Holtz. I'm sorry. I can't possibly take the job!

Questions

The discussion questions given in the student's book on page 5 should be used after listening to the dialogue.

The Interactive Listening ✳ 4

Tape: Part Four — Are you good at numbers?

There are three parts to this exercise. In the first part, I will read ten numbers. There is a list of ten numbers in your student's book on page 6. Your job is to compare the number I read with the written one. If they are the same, just put a check next to the number in your book. If they're different, cross out the incorrect number and put the correct one next to it.

1. $24.11	2. $989.02	3. $1,024.24	4. $1,545.25	5. $1,045.25
6. $1,087.24	7. $56.00	8. $2,000,650.00	9. $123,456.78	10. $500,000.00

In the second part of this exercise, I will read you five numbers. Take them in dictation.

1. $6,666.16   2. $.15   3. $90.19   4. $10,000,000   5. $100,100.10

In the third part of the exercise, we are again at the bank where Freddy works. Our interviewer, Ed, has come back to the bank the next day because he has a banking problem. It's a common problem: his checkbook doesn't balance. Listen now, along with Freddy, to Ed and see if you can find the mistake or mistakes in his checkbook (on page 7 in your student's book) and make corrections.

INTERVIEWER. Hi Freddy. And again, thank you for taking the time yesterday for the interview.

FREDDY. No problem.

INTERVIEWER. Well, but I've got a problem, a money problem, and I hope that you can help me. I'm having a terrible time balancing my checkbook this month. I feel so dumb, but I understand that your bank has a new service which helps customers like me who have this trouble.

FREDDY. We do. You'd be surprised how many people come in for our help with checkbook balancing. Why don't you give me your bank book and we can go over it together while you describe the transactions for me.

INTERVIEWER. All right. Here it is. Now, as you can see, at the beginning of the month I had a balance of four hundred and seventy six dollars. Now I know that's right. Then, I didn't write any checks as you can see, and I didn't make any deposits until March 14. That's when I got paid, and I came and deposited my check into my account. You see, there that is. So at that point, let's see, I had a thousand and ninety-nine dollars.

FREDDY. So far, so good.

INTERVIEWER. Then, while I was depositing my paycheck, I took out fifty dollars. Two days later, I wrote the telephone company a check for forty-seven dollars. See, I've got that right here. Then, my Aunt Lil sent me a birthday check, and I deposited that . . . see, that's here . . . birthday check. Now, where were we, where are we? Then, I bought some things at the bookstore for twenty-five eleven and also took out a hundred dollars cash. Here. Then I paid by check at the supermarket and then I got my paycheck again, deposited it, and took out fifty dollars. Then I got a refund of ten dollars from state tax and deposited it. There. But here's the problem. Now, there is almost a two hundred dollar difference in what I show here in my checkbook and in what the bank says I have. I think the bank's made a mistake.

FREDDY. Well, hmmm . . . let's see, my trusty little calculator. Actually, I'm sorry, sir, but I think you have made a mistake. As a matter of fact, a few of them.

Now, show Ed what his checkbook should be.

Answers to the interactive listening exercise

Part 1.

			Part 2.	
1. $24.11	✓		1. $6,666.16
2. $989.02	✓		2. $0.15
3. $1024.24	✓		3. $90.19
4. $1545.20	$1545.25		4. $10,000,000
5. $1042.25	$1045.25		5. $100,100.10
6. $10,876.24	$1087.24		
7. $.56	$56.00		
8. $2,000,065.00	$2,000,650.00		
9. $123,456.78	✓		
10. $5,000,000.00	$500,000.00		

Part 3.

CHECK NO.	DATE	CHECKS ISSUED TO OR DESCRIPTION OF DEPOSIT	(−) AMOUNT OF CHECK	✓ T	(−) CHECK FEE (IF ANY)	(+) AMOUNT OF DEPOSIT	BALANCE 476
121	3/14	paycheck				623 ··	623 / 1099
ABT	3/14	withdrawal	50 ··				50 / 1049
122	3/16	New England Telephone	47				47 / 1002 ··
Dep.	3/18	birthday check				100	100 / 1102 00
123	3/18	bookstore	25 11				25 11 / 1076 89
124	3/20	cash	100 ··				100 00 / 976 89
125	3/20	supermarket	26 28				26 28 / 950 61
	3/21	paycheck				623 ··	623 ·· / 1573 61
ABT	3/21		50 ··				50 / 1523 61
	3/22	refund				10 ··	10 ·· / 1533 61

PLEASE BE SURE TO **DEDUCT** ANY PER CHECK CHARGES OR SERVICE CHARGES THAT MAY APPLY TO YOUR ACCOUNT

REMEMBER TO RECORD AUTOMATIC PAYMENTS / DEPOSITS ON DATE AUTHORIZED

The Projects

A choice of communicative activities

The projects are designed to be done concurrently with the listening work. The explanations for the projects start on page 8 of the student's book.

Lesson Two

Dolores Silva
Co-owner of a Small Business

Note to the teacher or tutor:

Students of English feel that it's important to listen to and learn to understand native speakers of English, and rightly so. In choosing our people for this book, we chose people with a broad range of accents, both regional and ethnic. One American accent which foreign visitors often encounter and usually have great difficulty understanding is that of Hispanic Americans. Neither Dolores nor Tomas Martin are native speakers, although Dolores has lived in the Northeast of the United States for over thirty years. Like many immigrant Americans from all over the world, she has hung on to her accent. So, to represent these non-native Americans and to give our students the chance to become familiar with one of the most widespread ethnic accents both in Canada and in the United States, we included Dolores.

The issues involved with all the interpersonal relations Dolores is grappling with at this time are issues which most Canadians, Europeans, and Americans are concerned about. You may be surprised, as we have been, to find that many students, particularly men, from other parts of the world are simply not aware of the issues raised in this lesson.

Introductory Reading

This reading, which is given in the student's book on page 13, should be discussed as a prelistening exercise.

Work Related Vocabulary — with definitions

1. a **co-owner**: a person who owns something with another person
2. a **business manager**: usually the person who controls the financial (money) activities of an organization or business
3. a **sales person**: a person who sells things, especially in a store
4. an **accountant**: a person whose profession is to inspect the financial books of people, organizations, or businesses.
5. a **janitor**: a person whose job it is to keep clean the public areas of apartment buildings, schools, businesses
6. **arts and crafts objects**: (usually) handmade objects representing the folk culture of a country
7. **wholesale**: the sale of goods in large quantities, usually at discounted prices
8. **to import**: to bring goods into a country from another country
9. **correspondence**: letters (personal or business)
10. **to go over the books**: to inspect financial records
11. a **spring sale**: an event in the springtime at which a company or store sells its goods at a lower price
12. **to make an offer**: to suggest a price which one will pay for something
13. a **special offer**: an unusual offer by the sales person of a low price which is of special benefit to the customer
14. a **bargain**: something well worth the price that is paid; usually this price appears to be lower than its usual price
15. **profit**: the amount of money that remains after all the expenses have been paid
16. **profit margin**: the difference between the cost and selling price of goods or services sold
17. **retail**: the sale of goods in small amounts to the final customer; the opposite of wholesale
18. **inventory**: the goods or materials a company has in stock

Additional vocabulary

1. **to overwhelm**: to overcome completely; to overpower
2. a **variety**: a number of different types of things
3. **gruff**: rough and unpleasant; harsh
4. **the flu**: an abbreviation for the illness influenza
5. **dumb**: not clever or bright or intelligent. Not a kind term since dumb literally means unable to speak.
6. **to apologize**: to say "I am sorry for what I did or said."
7. **persuasion**: using words or other means to convince someone else to agree with you or to accept your point of view
8. **to skip lunch**: not to have lunch
9. **to unload**: to get rid of
10. a **cough**: to expel air from the lungs suddenly with a noise (often associated with a cold or influenza)

21

The Interview ✳ 1

Tape: Part One — The first listening

Lesson Two of People at Work begins with an interview with business woman, Dolores Silva. Before listening, review the work related vocabulary on page 14 in your student's book. You will listen to the interview at least twice. After the first listening, answer the questions in your book and then do the vocabulary in context exercise, using both your book and this tape. When you have finished the vocabulary in context, rewind and listen to the interview with Dolores again. We are in the Silva Enterprises gift shop. Ed, who has an appointment to meet Mrs. Silva, has entered and has been looking around at some of the interesting items in the store. Listen. Ed has found a marimba, and he's playing it, trying it out. He doesn't see Mrs. Sylva enter from the back room. Now Dolores Silva, co-owner of a small business.

DOLORES. That sounds wonderful!

INTERVIEWER. Really?

DOLORES. Yes. It's so good to hear someone play it. It really has a beautiful sound, don't you think?

INTERVIEWER. Oh, I agree. It's beautiful! You must be Dolores Silva.

DOLORES. That's right. And you must be the person who called about the interview.

INTERVIEWER. Yes. Now you *are* the owner of the store, Mrs. Silva, is that right?

DOLORES. Well, actually, my husband and I own it together, so I am the co-owner.

INTERVIEWER. Uh huh, co-owner. I thought that you were ... well, never mind. And you do have others working for you, is that right?

DOLORES. No, as you can see it's a small business. My husband and I do all the work ourselves, which means that I have to do a lot of different things. I am the business manager. I am the secretary, a buyer sometimes, often a salesperson. I am the accountant ....

INTERVIEWER. .... janitor?

DOLORES. Yes, especially janitor!

INTERVIEWER. Wow, it sounds a bit overwhelming having to wear all those hats.

DOLORES. Yes, but I like it. I like the variety. And some days it's easy, and I'm doing just one thing. Like today. I have been spending the whole day on the phone talking to buyers for gift shops. About marimbas, actually.

INTERVIEWER. If I remember correctly, you told me on the phone that you import arts and crafts objects and sell them wholesale to gift shops in the city, is that right?

DOLORES. Yes, that's right. We import mostly from Mexico but also from Central and South America.

INTERVIEWER. And you don't sell retail at all.

DOLORES. No. What you see here is just a showroom for the wholesale buyers.

INTERVIEWER. Uh huh. O.K. Now, back to what you do during the day. I guess there are easy days and the very busy days.

DOLORES. You've got it. For example, tomorrow should be easy. I'm planning to type correspondence in the morning; then I hope to go over the books in the afternoon. It should be an easy day. But that's the thing about this business; you really can't predict. There are those days when you just go crazy.... like yesterday. Oh, well, you don't want to hear about that.

INTERVIEWER. No, that's exactly what I do want to hear about. It'll give me a good idea of what you do here.

DOLORES. Well, O.K, here it is. It was one of those days. I had to do so many different things ... First of all, Ben—that's my husband—woke up sick, with a stomachache, ... some kind of flu. So I had to be the nurse and take his temperature and give him aspirin. Then I was a cook and fixed him some nice dry toast and some tea. Then, of course, I was the loving wife and kissed him goodbye.

INTERVIEWER. That's a lot of hats already. So then you were alone here all day.

DOLORES. Yes, and I got here to the store and it started out as an average kind of day: I opened the mail, paid a few bills, started work on the inventory, then I made some coffee, and all hell broke loose. Both phones started ringing. I picked up the first phone, and a man said he wanted to speak to the business manager. I had to put him on hold, so I could answer the second phone. And here was this awful man with this ugly, gruff voice. I immediately didn't like him. He said he owned a gift shop, and he wanted to make a business appointment with the owner of the company. I'm not exactly sure why, but he intimidated me, so when he said, "You are the secretary, aren't you?" I said, "yes."

INTERVIEWER. Well, it's true. You are the secretary.

DOLORES. Yes, but I'm also the owner, well the co-owner. I felt so dumb that I didn't tell him that. Then he said he wanted to come by the office at 3:30 that afternoon to look at our inventory, and I said sure and he could meet one of the owners then.

INTERVIEWER. Ah, so you knew that he'd come and realize that the secretary — the person on the phone — and the owner [are the same person].

DOLORES. [are the same person] I felt so dumb. He hung up, and I got back to the first phone. It was a Mr. Tomas Martin calling from Mexico. Can you imagine, and he'd been on hold for three minutes. He was very polite and he said he was calling about the marimbas. "Marimbas?" I asked him. "Yes, you know," he said, "the 200 marimbas you ordered last week, during our Spring sale." I couldn't believe my ears. 200 marimbas. "Are you sure?" I asked him. "Oh yes," he said. "I have the purchase order right here. But," he said, "the reason I'm calling is to make a special offer: I sell you 250 marimbas for the price of 200. It is a terrific bargain. There is almost no profit margin at all for me."

INTERVIEWER. But 250 marimbas? How in the world could you possibly sell ...?

DOLORES. Exactly. No way. It was crazy. What was my husband thinking about when he ordered 200 marimbas? I couldn't believe it. We haven't been able to sell this one. Naturally, I turned down his offer for the other fifty.

INTERVIEWER. That's easy to understand. So, here you were suddenly with 200 marimbas.

DOLORES. Yes, and I began to feel compulsive about selling them, so I got right on the phone, and the rest of the morning I was trying to sell them to retail stores, and I must say, with just a little bit of feminine charm, I did manage to unload twenty-five.

INTERVIEWER. Unload! You don't think much of those marimbas, do you?

DOLORES. Marimba ... carimba. O.K., then in the afternoon, I wrote a lot of letters to gift shops, and I described these beautiful, handmade Mexican marimbas ... such very unusual gifts.

INTERVIEWER. Well, they are.

DOLORES. Of course, they are. Now, at exactly 3:30, in walked the man with the gruff voice. Was he surprised to find that I, a mere women, am one of the owners. He was here for over an hour and, of course, bought nothing. And you know, I don't think he even recognized my voice.

INTERVIEWER. And he didn't buy a marimba?

DOLORES. He sniffed at the marimbas. After he left, I cleaned up the office and went home with a terrible headache.

INTERVIEWER. ... and your husband?

DOLORES. Oh my husband was fine, but he hadn't eaten all day, so of course he was very hungry. Well, I was exhausted, and I told him he had to be the cook, also the nurse!

INTERVIEWER. Also a marimba player, right?

DOLORES. Right. Also a marimba player.

INTERVIEWER. Hey, let me have another look at that marimba.

DOLORES. That beautiful, unusual, Mexican marimba?

INTERVIEWER. The same. Well, you know, secretly, I've always wanted a marimba. And maybe this is just the opportunity I've been looking for to pick up a real bargain. Huh? Would you hand me those sticks, please. Thanks.

DOLORES. That's beautiful. I think this marimba has found a new home.

INTERVIEWER. Well, you might convince me.

DOLORES. ... and what about those 174 others? For family and friends. They make wonderful birthday or Christmas gifts. I'll sell them to you cheap. No profit margin at all.

23

Questions

The general comprehension questions which are given in the student's book on page 15 should be discussed after the first listening to the interview.

Vocabulary in Context ✳ 2

Tape: Part Two — Listening exercise

Listen to this recording and write down the word or phrase you hear. You will hear the word or phrase twice. Then, listen to two sentences in which that word or phrase is used. The second sentence is taken from the conversation you have just heard. Next, write down what you think that word or phrase means. Make an intelligent guess, using context clues.

1. **to wear many hats**   to wear many hats
   Example: I wear many hats every day: I'm a father, a husband, a teacher, a friend . . . so many things.
   From the tape: It sounds a bit overwhelming having to wear all those hats.

2. **all hell broke loose**   all hell broke loose
   Example: After the man yelled "fire" in a large store, all hell broke loose as people screamed and ran and pushed.
   From the tape: All hell broke loose. Both telephones began ringing.

3. **to put [a telephone call] on hold**   to put [a telephone call] on hold
   Example: Excuse me. The other line of my telephone is ringing. May I put you on hold?
   From the tape: I had to put him on hold so I could answer the second phone.

4. **to believe one's ears**   to believe one's ears
   Example: When I heard that my new friend has twelve brothers and fourteen sisters, I couldn't believe my ears.
   From the tape: I couldn't believe my ears. Two hundred marimbas!

5. **to turn down**   to turn down
   Example: I got the job, but I turned it down because they didn't offer me enough money.
   From the tape: Naturally, I turned down his offer for the extra fifty [marimbas].

6. **to sniff at**   to sniff at
   Example: I thought it was a very good idea, but Mary just sniffed at it and said: "Try again!"
   From the tape: He sniffed at the marimbas.

Definitions of vocabulary in context

1.   to do many different kinds of jobs and functions
2.   great confusion and chaos developed
3.   to delay a phone call by asking someone to wait on the phone
4.   to believe what a person hears
5.   to reject; to refuse an offer
6.   to be critical of something and to reject it

24

The Interview ✳ 1

Tape: Part One, again — The second listening

Rewind the tape and listen to the interview again. Then answer the following questions and do the reconstruction exercise.

Detailed Questions

These detailed comprehension questions may be asked after the second listening to the interview. They do not appear in the student's book.

1. Silva Enterprises. What is their business?
2. Why wasn't Mr. Silva at work yesterday?
3. Dolores wears many hats. Explain in detail.
4. How did Dolores feel about the marimbas?
5. Can you remember how she attempted to sell the marimbas?
6. What did the interviewer think about the marimbas? Explain your answer.
7. 174. What is this number?
8. "He sniffed at the marimbas." Who is Dolores talking about, and what does she mean?
9. How did Dolores feel when she got home?
10. What are the pleasures and difficulties of Dolores's work?
11. What do you learn about the interviewer?

Reconstruction

The exercise which is given in the student's book on page 16 should be done after the second listening to the interview.

The Dialogue ✳ 1

Tapes: Part Three — A conversation between Dolores and Heftig

Listen to the conversation and then answer the questions in your book.

DOLORES. Silva Enterprises, good morning.

HEFTIG. Silva? What? Silva Enterprises? The importers?

DOLORES. Yes, sir.

HEFTIG. Lucas Heftig here. Look, I own a big shop down by the waterfront. You know where it is?

DOLORES. The waterfront? Yes, sir.

HEFTIG. No, no, I mean the gift shop. Rings and Things, that's the name of it.

DOLORES. Oh.

HEFTIG. Rings and Things, got it? See, I sell everything down there. . . .

DOLORES. I see. . . .

HEFTIG. Old stuff, new stuff, cheap, expensive; you name it, I sell it. You never heard of the place?

DOLORES. Uh . . . No, sir, I'm afraid not.

HEFTIG. Well, it doesn't matter anyway. The point is, see, I'm big. I'm one of the biggest in the city, know what I mean?

DOLORES. Indeed, sir.

HEFTIG. I do a lot of wholesale business to the small shops. I mean, sure, I also sell retail to the individual customers, but basically, uh, you know, I deal in quantity, all right?

DOLORES. I understand, sir.

HEFTIG. So. Like, do you have anything that would interest me? Gifts, cheap jewelry, that kind of stuff.

DOLORES. Well, our inventory is small, but interesting.

HEFTIG. Yeah?

DOLORES. We import primarily from Central and South America. We try to sell. . . .

HEFTIG. O.K., honey, that sounds fine. I got the picture basically. So look now, uh, when can I talk to the owner? I mean you're the secretary, right?

DOLORES. I . . . uh . . . well, yes . . . .

HEFTIG. So when can I see the boss man, huh?

DOLORES. (*Collecting herself*) Well, perhaps one of the owners could see you this afternoon. Would 3:30 be convenient?

HEFTIG. Sure, why not? Any time's good for business, right? Ha ha. So who will I talk to then, sweetheart?

DOLORES. (*Icily*) Just ask the secretary for Silva, sir.

HEFTIG. Beautiful, sweetheart. Thanks. Mr. Silva at 3:30.

DOLORES. Actually, sir, it will be . . . .

HEFTIG. O.K., honey, goodbye now. (*Hangs up.*)

DOLORES. (*Angrily, to herself*) Actually, it will be *Mrs.* Silva, sweetheart!

Questions

The discussion questions given in the student's book on page 17 should be used after listening to the dialogue.

The Interactive Listening 4

Tape: Part Four — Taking an order by phone.

Several months have passed. Once again Dolores gets a call from Tomas Martin in Mexico. Listen in on her conversation and, as she gives her order to Tomas, fill out his order form, which is given in your student's book on page 18.

(The phone rings. Dolores answers it.)

DOLORES. Good morning. Silva Enterprises. This is Dolores Silva speaking.

TOMAS. Hi, Dolores. This is Tomas Martin calling from Mexico to see if you can use some of our stock for your pre-Christmas sale.

DOLORES. Probably, Mr. Martin. What have you got? I'll see what we need.

TOMAS. OK. Fine. Well, we have some of those handknitted woolen hats from Chile, the ones that tie around the chin? You bought some last year.

DOLORES. Oh, yes.

TOMAS. We have them in two sizes, children's and adult's. They're four dollars apiece for the children's size and five dollars, fifty cents each for the adult size. If you buy them by the dozen, they are forty dollars a dozen for the children's hats and fifty five a dozen for the adult hats.

DOLORES. Fine. I remember them from last year. We sell a lot of them around Christmas in this cold climate. Why not give me a dozen of the adult size and a dozen and a half of the — well, no, no — make that two dozen of the children's.

TOMAS. Good! This year we also have some handknitted sweaters from Chile. They go with the hats, and they are the prettiest we've ever had. The children's sizes cost fourteen apiece — a real bargain. Both the men's style and the women's cost eighteen apiece. You can't beat those prices. As usual, they all come in small, medium, and large sizes.

DOLORES. I'll try two of the children's, two women's and two men's in each of the sizes. If they sell fast, I'll order more.

TOMAS. We have some wonderful leather handbags from Brazil that wholesale at forty-five dollars each. They are . . .

DOLORES. Sorry. Sorry. By the time I mark that up, it is more than my customers usually spend. Do you have any smaller items? Something to put into the Christmas stockings?

TOMAS. Well, let me see. We have some hand-painted coffee mugs from Mexico, some of the blue ware from Michoacan that you've bought before. You can have those at two dollars each or seventeen a dozen.

DOLORES. *(laughs)* Well, they're not exactly what I'd put in a stocking, but I'll take three dozen.

TOMAS. How about some small wooden boxes with animals painted on them. You can have them for only sixty cents each as long as you take a hundred of them.

DOLORES. I guess I'll pass on that. I still have a few. How about some dolls?

TOMAS. Sorry. None at the moment. I'll call you if and when they come in. We do have some of those blue lace tablecloth and napkin sets from Guatemala that you bought last summer. They're eight dollars a set.

DOLORES. I'll take five. They are so pretty and delicate. Anything else?

TOMAS. Well, we still have some of those marimbas on sale.

DOLORES. *(laughing)* Marimbas? Oh, no. No! Not marimbas! I never want to see, hear, touch, or play a marimba again!

Answers to the interactive listening exercise

Martin & Frank
Export/Import
Regalos Typicos Native Arts & Crafts

ORDER FORM. SEASON: CHRISTMAS ORDER DATE: PURCHASE ORDER #

ITEM	Quantity	Price/item	Special price	Total
ties (knit)				
ties (printed)				
hats (children)	2 dozen	$4.00 ea.	$40/dozen	$80.
hats (adults)	1 dozen	$5.50 ea.	$55/dozen	$55.
sweater (child sm.)	2	$14.00 ea.		$28.
sweater (" medium)	2	"		$28.
sweater (" large)	2	"		$28.
sweater (men sm.)	2	$18.00 ea.		$36.
sweater (" medium)	2	"		$36.
sweater (" large)	2	"		$36.
sweater (women sm.)	2	$18.00 ea.		$36.
sweater (" medium)	2	"		$36.
sweater (" large)	2	"		$36.
skirts				$36.
woven handbags				
leather bags	—	$45 ea.		
leather wallets				
coffee mugs (red)				
coffee mugs (blue)	3 dozen	$2.00 ea.	$17/dozen	$51.
3 bowls, set (red)	—		$60/c	
boxes (animals)				
tops (animals)				
picture frames				
dolls (Mexican)	call if they come in			
tablecloth set	5	$8.00/set		$40.
marimbas	—			
rattles (gourd)				
rattles (wood)				
belt buckles				
creche figures				
5 tree ornaments				
			TOTAL	$526

The Projects

A choice of communicative activities

The projects are designed to be done concurrently with the listening work. The explanations for the projects start on page 19 of the student's book.

Lesson Three

Neal Wade
Waiter

Note to the teacher or tutor:

Neal is a waiter, and a good one, but like Freddy Gallagher, Neal's job is just a means to an end. He is successful as a waiter and he is trying hard to succeed at his true vocation, acting.

There are many, many issues you and your class could discuss relating to this lesson. They may want to discuss funding for the arts, but they will be more *likely to focus on the vocabulary and culture of the restaurant, particularly if they haven't done so already in an earlier class. The menu provides you with a good piece of realia around which to build discussions and perhaps role-plays. (For an explanation of this technique see* Language Teaching Techniques *from Pro Lingua Associates.)*

Introductory Reading ✿

This reading, which is given in the student's book on page 21, should be discussed as a prelistening exercise.

Work Related Vocabulary — with definitions

1. a **bus boy**: a helper for the waiter
2. **tips**: money left for the waiter by the customer
3. a **fridge**: slang for refrigerator
4. a **flexible schedule**: a schedule that can be changed easily
5. a **shift**: one part of a work schedule; the period when one worker or a group of workers are on duty
6. **time off**: resting time away from work
7. **prep work**: preparation work preceding the time when the restaurant opens.
8. to **set up the table**: to put the necessary eating utensils on the table — knives, forks, spoons, glasses, napkins
9. **specials**: special foods prepared for a particular day by the restaurant cooks
10. **bread warmers**: special small ovens where bread is kept warm.
11. **rare meat**: the meat is cooked only a short time
12. **well-done meat**: the meat is cooked through until it is quite completely browned
13. an **order of fries**: a serving of french fried potatoes
14. **stressful job**: a job in which the person feels emotional, physical, mental tension or pressure
15. **decaf**: usually coffee without caffeine (a stimulant found in coffee and tea)

Additional vocabulary

1. a **run**: a length of time during which a theatrical work is performed. If it closes after a short period of time, it is said to have had "a short run."
2. **iffy**: from the word "if"; risky
3. to **cater to**: to try to please others by serving their needs.

The Interview 1

Tape: Part One — The first listening

Lesson Three of People at Work begins with an interview with waiter, Neal Wade. Before listening, review the work related vocabulary on page 22 of your student's book. You will listen to the interview at least twice. After the first listening, answer the questions in your book and then do the vocabulary in context exercise, using both your book and this tape. When you have finished the vocabulary in context, rewind and listen to the interview with Neal again. Now, Neal Wade, waiter.

INTERVIEWER. Neal, How did you happen to become a waiter?

NEAL. That's easy. I'm not qualified to do anything else.

INTERVIEWER. Oh, come on now.

NEAL. No, I've tried different things, but waiting tables is really the only thing I could do.

INTERVIEWER. Well, what other things have you tried?

NEAL. I tried teaching English as a second language, like you, in Newark, New Jersey. I've been a painter and a carpenter and a baker, and I was in advertising ... in all this stuff, but it really didn't work. And waiting tables seemed the only thing I could do and get good money.

INTERVIEWER. How long have you been doing it?

NEAL. On and off since I was fourteen, when I got my first busboy job.

INTERVIEWER. So then you've worked in many different restaurants, different places ...?

NEAL. Oh yeah, and closed several of them.

INTERVIEWER. Closed ... you mean ...?

NEAL. Yeah, many that closed ... finished, stopped serving food, no more work. Goodbye ... adios.

INTERVIEWER. .... because ...?

NEAL. I think that most of the restaurants that would hire me in the first place would be ....

INTERVIEWER. .... be likely to close?

NEAL. Oh, yeah.

INTERVIEWER. Well, but seriously ...

NEAL. Well, basically, it's a very iffy business. But, in some cases, the restaurant closed because it wasn't very good, or because the customers got poisoned, or the weather was terrible for a long time so nobody came, a bad location — one got burned down because of the Mafia — or they just weren't very lucky. I was in some very good places that closed.

INTERVIEWER. Well, do you foresee a short run for the Fifth Season?

NEAL. No, I'm hoping that this one'll break the mold. The place hasn't been open very long, but it's good. I think it's got a good chance to survive.

INTERVIEWER. Do you like waiting?

NEAL. Oh sure. For one thing, waiting on tables is, economically, very practical because, number one, it's money right there; you get your tips every day and you can carry that money home with you ... and for another thing, you're in a restaurant ... you get to eat, nibble a little of this or that. My fridge at home is empty. I do my eating here. Also, I can have a very flexible schedule. If I need to, I can change from the lunch shift to the dinner shift, and I can always get someone to cover for me, if I want to have time off. Also, it's mindless, waiting tables.

INTERVIEWER. Mindless?

NEAL. Well, routine, anyway.

INTERVIEWER. Is that one of the things you like about it?

NEAL. Yes, frankly. I put my creative energies outside the restaurant.

INTERVIEWER. Outside ...?

NEAL. In theater ...

INTERVIEWER. You mean, like acting ... directing ... writing ... ?

NEAL. Acting ...

INTERVIEWER. Here in Brattleboro.

NEAL. Right.

INTERVIEWER. Huh, then maybe I've seen you in something, because I go to the theater a lot here.

NEAL. Did you see ... ?

INTERVIEWER. Wait, wait, wait. Don't tell me. Let me look at you a minute. Wait. Sure, weren't you in that hilarious *Noises Off* ... weren't you the drunk burglar?

NEAL. That's right.

INTERVIEWER. Oh, it was hilarious ... it's a wonderful play. And, of course, I loved you in it. But I didn't recognize you. I hadn't realized ...

NEAL. Yeah ... I think that was the best time I've ever had in the theater.

INTERVIEWER. But, of course, that's community theater, and you don't get paid for that, do you?

NEAL. No.

INTERVIEWER. So the theater, then, is your first love.

NEAL. Yup, you guessed it. Waiting is just a way of making a living. Eventually I want to work my way into a professional theater company. And full-time work.

INTERVIEWER. And, in the meantime, you continue to act with local groups. And you also perform here at the restaurant. What would be a typical performance here at the restaurant?

NEAL. Funny, you just said "typical performance."

INTERVIEWER. Well, this is theater here too, isn't it?

NEAL. Oh yes, pure theater. You come in, and you're on stage; and when I come in, if I've had a bad day, feel awful, that's got to switch off as soon as I walk in. The show must go on. But you want a typical day. O.K. I come in around four, have my dinner. Then we start the prep work, get the coffee ready, setting up the tables, finding out what the specials are, folding napkins, preparing the butter, putting the bread in the warmers.

31

INTERVIEWER. And all the waiters and waitresses do that.

NEAL. We all do. All the "wait people" do.

INTERVIEWER Oh, oh. All right.

NEAL. Then I'm ready to wait.

INTERVIEWER. And to earn your money.

NEAL. Right ... and here you have to earn your money ... and earning your money means taking care of people and serving people and being pleasant or whatever it is you sense these people need you to be. Do they want you to be servile, do they want you to be gregarious, or do they want you to enter in to their conversation or do they want you to be like another piece of the furniture? Maybe it's a business lunch. But you have to pick up on what's wanted. That's not easy, and that's why waiters very frequently burn out. Let's face it, sometimes you really don't care if someone wants his meat cooked rare or well done, and sometimes the cook doesn't get it right ....

INTERVIEWER. Yeah, right, but you have to care anyway.

NEAL. Yeah, you have to care ... and sometimes you get really rude people who will snap their fingers at you ... like that ... but for the waiter, the bottom line is, well, it's the money. You want to get that order right, you want to please the customer. There's that tip, and you're depending on that, face it.

INTERVIEWER. To go back a bit to something that you said before ... so you think that, what, say 95% of the time you can get tuned in to what your customer wants?

NEAL. Hey, I have to. Once in a while I miss, but that's because I've just not guessed right. And then once in a while you go nuts and you go in the kitchen and you scream. It's been documented that waiting tables is among the most stressful jobs. And it is. I mean, you have to put your own life away for awhile, being absolutely pleasant, making sure that all the food is coming out correctly, running around ... all of that combined is what makes this very difficult, because all you're doing is catering to other people's needs ... different people, with different moods, and you've gotta stay tuned in. It builds up to something that is very, very stressful. It isn't a complicated job, but ... oh ... sorry. I never asked you. I wasn't tuned in ... Could I get you something. Coffee? Tea? Decaf? Bread ... water ... how about a fish stick ...

INTERVIEWER. Why, let me see a your menu. I think I would like something to eat.

NEAL. If you'll promise not to snap your fingers at me. We've got a couple of great specials tonight. Want to hear what they are?

INTERVIEWER. My mouth is watering already.

Questions

The general comprehension questions which are given in the student's book on page 23 should be discussed after the first listening to the interview.

Vocabulary in Context 2

Tape: Part Two — Listening exercise

Listen to the recording and write down the word or phrase you hear. You will hear the word or phrase twice. Then, listen to two sentences in which that word or phrase is used. The second sentence is taken from the interview you have heard. Next, write down what you think the word or phrase means. Make an intelligent guess, using the context clues.

1. **On and off**   on and off
    Example: No, I don't go swimming at the Y every day, not even every week. I go … um … on and off.
    From the tape: How long have I been doing it? On and off, since I was fourteen.

2. **to cover for**   to cover for
    Example: I'm quite sick, and I know I can't get out of bed. I need to get someone to cover for me at work tonight.
    From the tape: I can always get someone to cover for me if I want to have time off.

3. **to switch off**   to switch off
    Example: Hey, when you leave the office tonight, would you please switch off the lights?
    From the tape: When I come in, if I've had a bad day, feel awful, that's got to switch off as soon as I walk in.

4. **to pick up on**   to pick up on
    Example: Now, if you're feeling sick and I don't pick up on it, be sure to tell me instead of suffering in silence.
    From the tape: But you have to pick up on what's wanted.

5. **to burn out**   to burn out
    Example: I've been working nonstop without any time off for three months, and I've lost interest in what I'm doing. I guess I'm really burned out.
    From the tape: That's not easy, and that's why waiters very frequently burn out.

6. **the bottom line**   the bottom line
    Example: You're right. I want a car, and this one is practical and economical. But the bottom line is I just don't have enough money right now to buy it.
    From the tape: But, for the waiter, the bottom line is the money.

Additional vocabulary

7. **to break the mold**   to break the mold
    Example: You really are a wonderful person … you are cleverer, funnier, prettier, more sensitive than anyone I know. You break the mold.
    From the tape: No, I hope that this one will break the mold.

8. **tuned in**   tuned in
    Example: I want to be tuned in to you. I want to know what you really are thinking and what you really are feeling.
    From the tape: Because all you're doing is catering to other people's needs … different people, with different moods, and you've got to stay tuned in.

Definitions of vocabulary in context

1. not at regular, specific times; occasionally
2. to replace; to do the work of someone else at that person's request.
3. to turn off; extinguish; stop using a switch, usually electrical or mechanical (here an imaginary emotional switch)
4. to listen to and then to react appropriately to
5. to become exhausted (here, because of stressful work)
6. finally, the most important and most significant point or idea or concern — a financial term meaning the ultimate total or profit.
7. to be very different from the usual (in a positive way).
8. to be listening very carefully and responding appropriately to what one hears

Vocabulary in Context 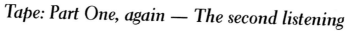 1

Tape: Part One, again — The second listening

Rewind the tape and listen to the interview again. Then answer the following questions and do the reconstruction exercise.

Detailed Questions

These detailed comprehension questions may be asked after the second listening to the interview. They do not appear in the student's book.

1. Why is Neal a waiter?
2. What are some of the other jobs Neal has had?
3. Neal tells about some restaurants he worked in that closed. What were the reasons for the closing of those restaurants?
4. The interviewer asks Neal: "Do you foresee a short run for the Fifth Season?" What is Neal's answer?
5. What does he say about his usual routine?
6. Does Neal like waiting on tables?
7. Where does Neal put his "creative energies"?
8. Can you describe what Neal says are the difficulties of being a waiter?
9. Neal and the interviewer seem to think that waiting has similarities to acting. Explain.
10. "The show must go on." What is Neal referring to?
11. Neal apologizes for not being "tuned in" to the interviewer. What does he mean, and what does he then suggest?
12. Describe how the interview ends.
13. What is your final impression of Neal? Do you think he is a good waiter? Why or why not? Do you think he'll be a waiter for a long time? Does he want to be a waiter for a long time?

Reconstruction

The exercise which is given in the student's book on page 24 should be done after the second listening to the interview.

The Dialogue ✳ 3

Tape: Part Three — A conversation between Neal and Louise

Listen to the conversation and then answer the questions in your book.

NEAL. One chicken cacciatori with french fries, one special with a baked potato, one chef salad — easy on the mayo.

LOUISE. Making a change. Change my beef stroganoff to the quiche with onions and a cup of pea soup.

COOK. Oh my God, not another change . . . .

NEAL. Hey, Louise, what's up? You look terrible.

LOUISE. Everything's just fine. It's just fine.

NEAL. It's not just fine. You're face is purple. You've been crying. What is it?

LOUISE. It's O.K., nothing.

NEAL. It's not O.K. Now, tell me what's bugging you.

LOUISE. Well, you know I've been on the edge all night, and there was this final straw ....

NEAL. Is it that macho guy at your table five?

LOUISE. How'd you know!

NEAL. I had him one night last week ... the one who snaps his fingers. Hand me that basket of rolls, would you. And where's the butter?

LOUISE. It's right there next to the shrimp. And not just snapped his fingers. First he growled at me because I didn't fill his water glass the second he sat down. And then there's this impossible woman with him ... she's even more obnoxious than he is. Well, she complained that the music was too loud and then she sent me running to get a different fork because she found lipstick on hers. Then five minutes later I come back, open the bottle of the wine he ordered, and she sniffs it and grouses that it's not the vintage he asked for.

NEAL. Hey, there must be a full moon. That's the kind of night I'm having. Everybody's grousing. Look ... relax, honey, relax. Damn, we've run out of the blue cheese.

LOUISE. Give me that tomato and that long knife, O.K.?

NEAL. The tomato, maybe, but I'm not giving you that long knife.

LOUISE. Neal, I wouldn't do that, would I!?

NEAL. Well, he deserves it. Here it is, but be careful!

LOUISE. .... but I'm not even finished. So later I bring him the beef stroganoff he ordered, and he says, "Look baby, I can't eat this garbage, bring me the quiche instead." By now I was so furious I was going to throw the beef stroganoff in his face. But I bit my lip and said, very cooly, "Yes, sir, of course, sir, but real men don't eat quiche." And I turned on my heels, and that's when he snapped his fingers. And, oh, here I am hiding.

NEAL. Oh, that's perfect ... real men don't eat quiche.

LOUISE. Of course, it's perfect. But I can't believe I said that. The customer is always right, isn't he? I mean, we know he isn't, but, good god ... I simply can't go back in there. I can't go to that table. And the other thing. You know my nine year old daughter is home sick tonight. And just before I left to come here, the baby sitter called and said she couldn't come. So there's my daughter at home alone and sick. I can't stand it. And now this. And I need this job! Could you hand me some more lettuce? One more of those small salad bowls ... thanks.

NEAL. Hey. Look, stop it. Look at me! I'm going to take over that table for you. I'm going to be delighted to take that slob his quiche.

LOUISE. Are you serious? Could you? ... Would you?

NEAL. I can, I will. No arguing. I've only got three tables right now. And listen, if you can last for about fifteen more minutes, I'll take over your other three tables too, so that you can get home early. No sweat. You should get home to that sick kid of yours.

LOUISE. You are a saint, Saint Neal. You get all of my tips tonight. You get all my tips forever.

COOK. Quiche with onions, chef salad with a side of fries.

NEAL. Well, Louise, wish me luck. And if he doesn't like the quiche, I'm snapping my fingers at him. And you'd better hide that long knife.

LOUISE. I can't believe this.

Questions

The discussion questions given in the student's book on page 25 should be used after listening to the dialogue.

The Interactive Listening 4
Tape: Part Four — Taking orders

The waitress, Louise, is waiting on four people who are having lunch at the Fifth Season. You are going to recognize some of these voices. Listen to their conversation and take down their orders on the checks supplied in your student's book on page 26. After you have checked out the prices on the menu, add up the bill for each person. Be sure to add the five percent state sales tax charged on all meals in this state.

ANDY. And what are you going to have, Matt?

MATT. Oh, I don't know. Something light, I guess. We're going to Annie's mother's for dinner tonight, and there's always a very heavy meal, if you know what I mean.

ED. Well, and just what do you mean by that!

MATT. Oh, you know what I mean.

ED. Well, all right.

ANDY. I think I'll go with the lunch special. Ah, here comes the waitress.

WAITRESS. Good afternoon. Can I get you anything to drink?

ANDY. How about a glass of white wine for everyone?

MATT, ELISE, ED. (simultaneously) That's fine, perfect, yes, that's what I want, sounds great to me . . . .

WAITRESS. Certainly. Can I interest you in our special of the day? We have soup and salad. The soup is a cream of asparagus, and it comes with a small chef salad for $2.95. And you can't beat that.

MATT. Sounds great. Then I won't eat anything else until I get to Annie's mother's house tonight. Andy?

ANDY. No waistline watching for me today. I think I'll start with the fresh fruit salad with orange sherbet. Then, I'm going to have that fresh fried shrimp and also some tea with lemon please.

WAITRESS. (to Matt) Did you want something to drink with your soup and salad?

MATT. Yeah, you bet. How about some decaffinated coffee when you bring my salad. And what about you Elise? The usual salad?

ELISE. Listen, I've lost five pounds. So I'm going to have the tunafish salad plate with some oil and vinegar on the side. And some black coffee.

WAITRESS. . . . . (writing) . . . and black coffee. And you, sir?

ED. Oh, the hell with diets. I'll have the turkey club sandwich with a side order of fries and a large chef salad, and lots and lots of heavy, heavy blue cheese dressing. And for dessert — I'm going to order my dessert right now because I've been thinking about it all morning — I'll have your wonderful "Death by Chocolate."

ELISE. How decadent.

ANDY. How obscene.

MATT. How delicious.

WAITRESS. It's an excellent, excellent choice.

ED. And, do you have any diet drinks?

WAITRESS. We have Tab and Diet Coke.

ED. I'll have the Diet Coke.

MATT. Ed, you're crazy.

ELISE. Impossible . . .

WAITRESS. All right, I'll get your order here as soon as possible.

ANDY. And waitress, would you please bring us separate checks.

ED. Separate checks?

ANDY. Well . . .

Answers to the interactive listening exercise

MATT

wine	2.00
special	2.95
coffee	.55
Subtotal	5.50
Tax	.28
Total	5.78

ANDY

wine	2.00
fruit cup	1.00
fresh fried shrimp	5.50
tea	.55
Subtotal	9.05
Tax	.45
Total	9.50

ELISE

wine	2.00
tunafish salad platter	3.75
coffee	.55
Subtotal	6.30
Tax	.32
Total	6.62

ED

wine	2.00
turkey club	3.95
french fries	.75
large chef salad	1.50
blue cheese dressing	.25
death by chocolate	1.50
Diet Coke	.45
Subtotal	10.40
Tax	.52
total	10.92

The Projects

A choice of communicative activities

The projects are designed to be done concurrently with the listening work. The explanations for the projects start on page 28 of the student's book.

Lesson Four

Bertha Haynes
Elementary School Teacher

Note to the teacher or tutor:

The one variation in the Bertha Hayne's chapter is at the beginning. Before reading the introduction, students are asked to do a write-before-you-read exercise. Since students are often very anxious to read aloud and talk about what they have written, more than ten minutes should be given for this activity.

Write-before-You-Read

For ten minutes write freely about a teacher from your elementary or high school or even from your university whom you remember very well. This will not be collected, but you may share it aloud or talk about it if you wish to.

Introductory Reading

This reading, which is given in the student's book on page 33, should be discussed as a prelistening exercise.

Work Related Vocabulary — with definitions

1. **modified**: changed somewhat; altered for a purpose
2. an **open classroom**: an educational system for elementary and high school in which the student has a choice in his/her school activities and learning program
3. **Cherokee Indians**: a tribe of American Indians
4. a **pair of scissors**: an instrument for cutting paper and other objects
5. a **work contract**: an agreement about a study plan reached between the teacher and student
6. an **assignment**: the school work which needs to be done
7. a **learning disability**: generally, a problem in learning
8. **dyslexia**: a type of learning disability often involving a visual problem in the central nervous system. This problem often leads to difficulties in reading.
9. a **recess**: a short intermission between activities. In elementary school, it is usually a time for playing.
10. an **extended classroom**: a learning environment outside of the schoolroom

Additional vocabulary

1. **chaotic**: very confused and without order and a system
2. to **growl**: to utter a deep sound of anger or hostility from the throat. (A dog does this; a dog also barks.)
3. **tell me about it**: I know what you mean from personal experience
4. a **loom**: an instrument used in weaving
5. a **pattern**: a design
6. **cops**: policemen
7. a **beat**: a route taken by walking policemen
8. **strict**: guided by exact rules

The Interview ✳ 1

Tape: Part One — The first listening

Lesson Four of People at Work begins with an interview with teacher, Bertha Haynes. Before listening, review the work related vocabulary in your book on page 34 and do the write-before-you-read exercise. You will listen to the interview at least twice. After the first listening, answer the questions in your book and then do the vocabulary in context exercise, using both your book and the tape. When you have finished the vocabulary in context, rewind and listen to the interview again. We are in a busy fifth grade classroom in a public elementary school. The interviewer has just entered, and he approaches the teacher who is sitting in a corner watching the students work. Now, Bertha Haynes, elementary school teacher.

INTERVIEWER. Mrs. Haynes, I have to say in all honesty that this just isn't at all what I was expecting to see today.

BERTHA. What were you expecting?

INTERVIEWER. Well, the way I remember my fifth grade class, I guess I was expecting that you would be standing in front of the room and everyone would be looking at you and basically, I guess, that everyone would be doing the same thing and you would be the center of attention. This really surprises me.

BERTHA. Does it seem chaotic to you?

INTERVIEWER. No, not really. It's a wonderful beehive of activity: look at those two over there in the kitchen area cooking and baking, and those three boys over there quietly reading, and the girl working on the loom ... and all the others busy and interested in what they're doing. And here you stand talking with me, and they aren't paying any attention to you ... to us ... at all. They don't seem to need you. What blows me away is that it all seems so ... what's the word ... purposeful, I guess.

BERTHA. Purposeful. I think so. I hope so.

INTERVIEWER. Well, how does it happen? How do you do it?

BERTHA. I told you on the telephone, didn't I, that here at the James School we use a modified open classroom system.

INTERVIEWER. Open classroom, yeah, that's what you told me.

BERTHA. Now let me try to explain what's going on right now, and I think you'll get an idea about the open classroom. Let me begin by saying that two weeks ago we started working on a project on the Cherokee Indians, so all of our work, our reading, writing, science, geography, history, arithmetic, all of our classes are related to the Cherokee Indians — learning about their living conditions in the early 1800s.

MARY. Excuse me, Mrs. Haynes, I can't find our good pair of scissors.

BERTHA. Did you look on top of my desk?

KATY. They're not there.

BERTHA. Then look in the middle drawer of my desk ... or maybe Felix is using them.

KATY. O.K.

BERTHA. What was I saying?

INTERVIEWER. Cherokee Indians?

BERTHA. Oh, yes. So, you see, we have the class project, and what happens is that each student makes a work contract with me each week. In that contract, the student agrees to do a certain amount of work in all the major subject areas. Often the student works alone, sometimes with one, two or three others, or more, on a certain assignment related to the Cherokee Indian project. My job, then, is to work individually with them, or to coordinate the small-group work, to encourage them, to keep them on track. And, of course, to growl when that is necessary. Does that make any sense?

INTERVIEWER. Well, it makes sense. I just don't see how you do it. How could anyone do it? It just seems so complicated to me.

BERTHA. I'd be lying if I said it's easy. It isn't.

INTERVIEWER. Tell me about that little blond girl over there at the loom in the corner there.

BERTHA. That's Julie Clampit. Let's go over. She loves to weave. She'd do it all day if she could. At the beginning of the week we made a contract that she would work on the loom twice during the week. Hi, Julie. Mr. Smith is very interested in what you're doing. Tell him what you're making.

JULIE. Hi. It's a Cherokee Indian rug.

BERTHA. You see that pattern she's using. It's a Cherokee Indian pattern.

INTERVIEWER. Julie, it's beautiful work. How did you get to be so good at weaving.

JULIE. Well, we have a loom at home, and my mom teaches me things.

INTERVIEWER. Wow, it's beautiful.

BERTHA. Thank you, Julie, I don't want to interrupt you. Now let me show you the corner where the children do their art work. But let me finish about Julie. You can see how good she is at the weaving, and she's also very good at arithmetic. But the interesting thing is she has a terrible time with reading.

INTERVIEWER. My, that's surprising.

BERTHA. You see, she has a learning disability: she's dyslexic, and she's far behind the other students. So I can't and don't expect as much from Julie in reading as I do from the other students.

KATY. Mrs. Haynes, Felix keeps taking my paint brush and pulling my hair. Tell him to stop it.

FELIX. Well . . . she keeps calling me fat face.

KATY. I do not!

BERTHA. Now, Katy and Felix, you know what we've said about this. Keep on with your art work now, and we'll have a little conference during recess.

INTERVIEWER. Well, I guess no system is perfect.

BERTHA. Well, as you've probably heard, children aren't always perfect.

INTERVIEWER. Oh, well, tell me about it! Oh, I know what I wanted to ask you. Didn't I see you with your class down by the police station last week? Tuesday, I think it was.

BERTHA. And you wondered why we weren't back in the school.

INTERVIEWER. Well, I wondered. But I was cleverly guessing that you probably like to use the whole city as a kind of extended classroom. Right?

BERTHA. Exactly. Good for you. Before we started on our Cherokee Indian project, we were doing a project on policemen. The kids learned about a policeman's life by reading the police reports, riding in police cars, and even walking with the cops on their beats. They learned that the problems of the police are the problems of the whole city. They investigated their own attitudes about policemen and police women and wrote down their feelings.

INTERVIEWER. My gosh, school is so very different from what it was when I was in fifth grade, lo these . . . thirty years ago. Gosh.

BERTHA. There are a lot of differences now. I hate to tell you, but I began teaching here at the James School twenty-two years ago, when I was twenty-six. But, of course, times do change, and educational methods and materials change. The rooms look different now too.

INTERVIEWER. Oh, when I was in grade school there were five rows of desks, six desks in a row, in a room and everything was nailed to the floor, and I usually just sat in the same place all day long. And teachers were so strict. Now, you've got these movable desks. Students move from place to place, and they write at these movable desks . . . It's so different.

BERTHA. We can be grateful for change.

INTERVIEWER. You've been teaching here for twenty-two years?

BERTHA. Yes.

INTERVIEWER. How can you have so much enthusiasm after all that time?

BERTHA. Enthusiasm? Well, strange as it may seem, I guess it's because I really love these kids. Most days, not every day, I have to admit, when I get up in the morning I wonder what wild, crazy things will happen. And with our open classroom system, there are a lot of surprises . . . and challenges for me.

KATY. Hey, Mrs. Haynes, do you and your friend wanna have some Indian bread. I just made it.

FELIX. Mrs. Haynes, you don't think I'm a fat face, do you?

41

Questions

The general comprehension questions which are given in the student's book on page 35 should be discussed after the first listening to the interview.

Vocabulary in Context ✷ 2

Tape: Part Two — Listening exercise

Listen to this recording and write down the word or phrase you hear. You will hear the word or phrase twice. Then, listen to two sentences in which that word or phrase is used. The second sentence is taken from the conversation you've just heard. Next, write down what you think that word or phrase means. Make an intelligent guess, using context clues.

1. **a beehive of activity**   **a beehive of activity**
   Example: When I went into the kitchen I found that it was a beehive of activity. My son and several of his friends were busy making bread and washing the dishes and cleaning the floor. I couldn't believe my eyes.
   From the tape: It's a wonderful beehive of activity.

2. **to blow [someone] away**   **to blow [someone] away**
   Example: Everytime I go to New York City and see all those tall buildings, it blows me away.
   From the tape: What blows me away is that it all seems so . . . . . . purposeful.

3. **on track**   **on track**
   Example: If I forget why I'm writing this book and I get discouraged, my partner always encourages me and gets me back on track.
   From the tape: My job, then, is to . . . encourage them, to keep them on track.

Definitions of vocabulary in context

1. a place where there is a great amount of productive, purposeful, and positive activity (as one would see in the house of bees)
2. to surprise very much; to astonish
3. the place where a person wants or needs to be in order to fulfill a plan or schedule

The Interview ✺ 1

Tape: Part One, again — The second listening

Rewind the tape and listen to the interview again. Then answer the following questions and do the reconstruction exercise.

Questions

These detailed comprehension questions may be asked after the second listening to the interview. They do not appear in the student's book.

1. The interviewer is surprised by what he sees in Bertha's classroom. What are the surprises?
2. Describe the interviewer's fifth grade room as he remembers it.
3. Describe the current class project in Bertha's room in as much detail as possible.
4. What is a work contract in Bertha's class?
5. What did you learn about Julie Clampit? (mention the loom, a learning disability, dyslexia ...)
6. How many children did you hear? Describe them as completely as possible. What were they talking about?
7. What is going to happen during recess today?
8. What example is given about the "extended classroom"? Describe Bertha's police project as fully as possible.
9. How old is Bertha?
10. You have heard some things about the open classroom system. From what you have heard, tell as much as you can about what this system is. What further questions would you want to have answered about the open classroom system?
11. Bertha believes that her teaching experience is quite different from what it was twenty-two years ago. How many of those differences do you remember?
12. She explains how she keeps her enthusiasm. What does she say?
13. What do you believe would be some of the advantages and the disadvantages of the open classroom system?

Reconstruction

The exercise which is given in the student's book on page 36 should be done after the second listening to the interview.

The Dialogue ✳ 3

Tape: Part Three — A conversation between Bertha and Mr. Sears

Listen to the conversation and then answer the questions in your book.

MR. SEARS. Mrs. Haynes?

MRS. HAYNES. Yes?

MR. SEARS. Uh, I'm . . . I'm the father of one of your new students.

MRS. HAYNES. Oh, how nice. That would be . . . .

MR. SEARS. Barry Sears is his name.

MRS. HAYNES. Barry? Oh, a delightful boy! Come in, Mr. Sears. It's nice to meet you.

MR. SEARS. I hope I'm not disturbing you. I know you're busy.

MRS. HAYNES. Not at all. We like new parents to drop by for a chat.

MR. SEARS. Well, I just wanted to check up on Barry's progress.

MRS. HAYNES. Oh, Barry's doing just fine, really.

MR. SEARS. He is?

MRS. HAYNES. Yes indeed. Most boys and girls have some trouble with a new school, but Barry is doing really excellent work.

MR. SEARS. Really? I was wondering . . . he never brings home much homework.

MRS. HAYNES. (*Laughs*) Well, that means he's completing his contracts during school hours. It means he's working very hard. He's a well-motivated boy, Barry is.

MR. SEARS. Gee, when I was in sixth grade *my* teacher gave me a *lot* of homework.

MRS. HAYNES. Well, educational theory changes constantly, you know.

MR. SEARS. Sure, but . . . math problems! History facts! She really made us work.

MRS. HAYNES. Yes, and you probably did a lot of memory work, too.

MR. SEARS. Memory work! We memorized everything! Kings and queens! Dates! Spelling lists!

MRS. HAYNES. Of course, there is a place for that.

MR. SEARS. Oh, yes, I'm sure there is.

MRS. HAYNES. But, we believe there are more important things. And more exciting methods.

MR. SEARS. Well, I can see that. I mean, homework for the sake of . . . .

MRS. HAYNES. . . . homework. Yes, and memory work. It's a little old-fashioned.

MR. SEARS. And behavior! Do you know what my teacher did when I behaved badly?

MRS. HAYNES. No, what?

MR. SEARS. She pulled my ears!

MRS. HAYNES. (*Laughs*) Oh, my, she sounds very strict.

MR. SEARS. She certainly was! She was a great teacher, though. Her name was Bertha Haynes.

MRS. HAYNES. (*Shocked pause*) I beg your pardon?

MR. SEARS. Mrs. Haynes, take a closer look at me. Twenty-two years ago, I was a student in your first class.

MRS. HAYNES. Wait a minute. You're not . . . oh, you can't possibly be . . . .

MR. SEARS. Yes, I am. I'm Phil Sears.

MRS. HAYNES. (*Amazed, amused*) Why, Phillip Sears! You devil! I ought to pull your ears! Do you mean to tell me that little Barry is your *son*?

MR. SEARS. Yes, ma'am.

MRS. HAYNES. I don't believe it! Oh, my goodness, that makes me feel old!

MR. SEARS. Makes *you* feel old? How do you think *I* feel? All the homework I did! All the memorizing! And now you tell me it's old-fashioned!

Questions

The discussion questions given in the student's book on page 37 should be used after listening to the dialogue.

The Interactive Listening 4

Tape: Part Four — Ed gets interviewed, and so do you.

For this exercise you meet Dr. Marilyn Jones. Marilyn is the principal of the James Elementary School where Bertha is the fifth grade teacher. She is also a good friend of Ed, our interviewer, who has just finished talking with Bertha. They meet in the hall outside Bertha's classroom. As you listen in on the conversation between Marilyn and Ed, take notes on her questions in your student's book on page 38.

MARILYN. Ed. Oh, you did come to visit Bertha.

INTERVIEWER. Oh, hi, Marilyn, oh yeah! Sure I did.

MARILYN. How did it go?

INTERVIEWER. Well, she was wonderful. And you were right. She's just what I needed for the book. And I want to thank you for making that possible. It's good to have friends in high places, you principal, you.

MARILYN. No problem. But . . . do you have a minute right now, before you trot off? I mean, just a minute.

INTERVIEWER. Sure.

MARILYN. I want to interview you.

INTERVIEWER. Well, that seems only fair.

MARILYN. I'm doing a very informal study this week and I'd like your input. I would like to ask you just three or four questions about your elementary school experience. So, if you've got just a minute . . . .

INTERVIEWER. O.K., sure, shoot.

MARILYN. First of all, where did you go to elementrary school?

INTERVIEWER. Well, that one's easy. It was out in Minnesota, in Alexandria, Minnesota.

MARILYN. So you're from Minnesota!

INTERVIEWER. Right.

MARILYN. I love those lakes out there. But those winters, brrrr!

INTERVIEWER. I hear you.

MARILYN. Next. When did you enter first grade?

INTERVIEWER. Oh, now, can I remember back that far? Come on, well, let's see, I guess it must have been 1932. I would have been six years old, and I was born in 1926. So that makes it the fall of 1932.

MARILYN. I hadn't realized that you are so . . . .

INTERVIEWER. . . . . so old!

MARILYN. I wasn't going to say that.

INTERVIEWER. Well, good. Thank you. Next question.

MARILYN. Another easy one. Was your elementary school co-educational?

INTERVIEWER. Oh, yes, it was. My guess is that boys and girls have always studied together in the public schools in Minnesota. I believe that a hundred years ago and before that, in the small towns, you would have a one room school house, and you had all the boys and girls from all the grades studying together in one room and with one teacher.

MARILYN. Did you wear uniforms?

INTERVIEWER. No, we didn't. We wore what we wanted to, and our mothers sent us off to school every day in neat and clean clothes, and we would come home in dirty clothes. But no, no uniforms.

MARILYN. O.K. Next question. Can you remember in which grade you learned to read?

INTERVIEWER. Hm. Not so easy. But if I remember correctly, it probably was in first grade, when I was six, seven years old. I'd probably learned the alphabet in kindergarten, or before kindergarten, but I think it was in first grade that I actually started to read real books, what I thought of as real books anyway, childrens' books, of course.

MARILYN. Um hum. Now about recess. Can you remember what you did during recess and how long the recess time was?

INTERVIEWER. Hm. Well, I think we used to have it in the middle of the morning — I suppose around 10:30 — and if it was the spring or fall, we'd go outside and I remember the girls jumping rope or the boys and the girls playing kickball, something like that. But, in the wintertimes, with all the snow and cold of Minnesota, I believe we stayed inside and we played games in our classroom.

MARILYN. And how much time did you have for recess?

INTERVIEWER. Oh, I think it was about ten to fifteen minutes.

MARILYN. One last question. Tell me about a good experience that you remember from your elementary school days.

INTERVIEWER. Oh, you should never have asked. I could go on forever. But, you know, the first thing that comes to my mind is that day in third grade when our teacher, Miss Tindall, asked me and my dear friend, James Bundy, to put on our jackets, and she gave us some money, and she sent us way across town to buy some library paste that she needed for our art lesson in the afternoon. We were delighted, and we were gone for, oh, two or three hours on that wonderful spring day. Oh, and **of course**, I would have to say something about the fifth grade and our fifth grade teacher, Miss Arne, and when she chose Audrey Tanquist and me to be the Baltimore orioles in the bird program which we gave for our parents ... and I would also have to talk about that wonderful day in Second grade .... I'll never forget that day when ...

Now that you have listened to Marilyn's interview with Ed, you should have noted down her eight questions. I want you to answer these questions yourself, explaining your elementary school experience. And here are a few extra questions for you to take down. Be prepared to answer all of these questions, sharing information about yourself with your classmates. You should also be prepared to share what you have learned about Ed's school days.

9. Did you have one teacher each year or more than one?
10. Did you work at your own speed or did everyone do the same work at the same time?
11. What was your favorite subject?
12. Did you do a lot of memorizing?
13. Did you have a lot of homework to do?
14. What happened to you when you misbehaved?
15. How did you get to school?
16. Did you go home for lunch?
17. How long was your school day?
18. Was your school all academic work like "reading, writing, and arithmetic" or did you also have art, music, dance, and sports? Were these considered to be important parts of your education or "extra-curricular activities?"

The Projects

A choice of communicative activities

The projects are designed to be done concurrently with the listening work. The explanations for the projects start on page 38 of the student's book.

Lesson Five

Douglas Clegg
Folk Singer

To the teacher or tutor:

The format of this lesson is quite different. We wanted to fit in three of Douglas' good songs. We've made some suggestions of what you can do with them, but there are many possibilities. If your students enjoy working with these songs, more are available on tape. Or you could arrange a visit from the artist himself. He makes his living visiting schools, as well as coffee houses, roadside night spots, and shopping centers. And he is a gifted entertainer.

If any of your students have musical talent, let this lesson bring them out. Sharing songs and other music is a wonderful way to bridge cultural barriers.

Introductory Song

Lesson Five of People at Work begins with a song by folk singer, Douglas Clegg. The words to the song are given in your student's book, but first, before you read them, listen to the song and try to understand what Douglas is singing about. The song is titled, "Fill My Thirst."

Introductory Reading ✿

This reading, which is given in the student's book on page 42, should be discussed as a prelistening exercise.

Work Related Vocabulary — with definitions

1. a **gig**: a job for a small musical [usually rock, jazz or folk] group
2. Various musical instruments:

Additional vocabulary

1. a **hobby**: an activity which a person does outside of work; examples: collecting stamps, playing a musical instrument, raising flowers, etc.
2. a **trend**: a general, not specific, direction; style or vogue
3. a **garage sale**: a sale of a family's unwanted household items, usually held in the family garage
4. **après ski**: French expression meaning "after ski"
5. a **pawn shop**: a shop of a pawn broker whose business is to lend money at interest to a person who brings in personal property and leaves it at the store. The owner of that property can get it back if he returns and pays the pawn broker the money lent to him and the interest on that money. In the story that Douglas tells, he was able to buy the instruments at a very low price because the person who left them in the pawn shop never returned for them.
6. a **passion**: a great love or interest
7. to **snowball**: to increase in growth rapidly
8. **for a living**: to earn money to live on
9. to **last**: to go on or to continue in time

48

The Interview ✳ 1

Tape: Part One — The first listening

Now for our interview with Douglas. Before listening, review the work related vocabulary in your book on page 43. You will listen to the interview at least twice. After the first listening, answer the questions in your book and then do the vocabulary in context exercise, using both your book and this tape. When you have finished the vocabulary in context, rewind and listen to the interview with Douglas again. Now, Douglas Clegg, folk singer. We are in the kitchen of Douglas and Jane Clegg. Douglas has been cooking a lunch for the interviewer, and his wife has just left with the Clegg's 6-month-old son who was clearly ready for his midday nap. Douglas has just served the interviewer an unusual delicacy...

INTERVIEWER. Why, this is delicious. What is it?

DOUGLAS. It's a Dutch baby.

INTERVIEWER. .... hmm. A Dutch baby. I've never tasted a Dutch baby before. You know, actually, you're quite a cook. Very impressive. Do you do a lot of cooking?

DOUGLAS. I love to cook. When I cook I feel that I'm producing something... creating something. Didn't I tell you... my first jobs were in restaurants. I was a cook. It's interesting, but I know a lot of musicians who started out as cooks. I cooked for a living and played music as my hobby in those days ....

INTERVIEWER. .... and now you play music for your living and cook as your hobby.

DOUGLAS. That's right. It's an interesting trend. I also find that waiting and acting is a similar kind of connection. It seems that a lot of waiters are actors or are waiting to become full time actors.

INTERVIEWER. Hm. Waiters waiting ....

DOUGLAS. .... to act

INTERVIEWER. And maybe even actors who are waiting.

DOUGLAS. Wait a minute ... it's too confusing.

INTERVIEWER. And you're waiting right now for me to go and get on with this interview, aren't you. Well, so I will. For a starter, how did you get started with music? Was there music in your house ... in your family?

DOUGLAS. I thought you'd never ask. Well, we had a piano in the house. Both my father and mother played piano. She played classical music, and he played popular music from the 20's 30's and 40's — swing music. He used to entertain people in the bars when he was in the army ... not for money. The soldiers would put beers up on the piano for him, and then while he played, they'd sing ... oh, songs like "Shine on Harvest Moon", that type of thing.

INTERVIEWER. What about your mother? Did she play the piano a lot or not?

DOUGLAS. Not as often. See, she had five kids ....

INTERVIEWER. You and your brothers and sisters.

DOUGLAS. Just brothers. There were five brothers ... I was fourth.

INTERVIEWER. Well, were any of them serious about music?

DOUGLAS. Not as much. I had two step grandfathers, and both of them had left violins when they died. My oldest brother studied the violin, but he didn't stick with it very long. You know, the routine of having to practice. He wasn't cut out for that sort of thing. The second brother started piano but only lasted a few months. The third brother played the French horn later, but then I came along and was teaching myself things on the piano, starting at about four or five years old. I'd sit at the piano and try to learn things, and I'd watch my father play. Let me show you what it sounded like ("Shine on, shine on harvest moon, up in the sky ....")

INTERVIEWER. And he had that kind of that rolling bass there. What do you call that kind of thing?

DOUGLAS. Stride bass, I guess, it's called.

INTERVIEWER. It's great. Then did you take lessons, or ...?

49

DOUGLAS. Well, I started taking piano lessons when I was about seven, and I took, for about six years I guess. But my main interest in life really has always been music.

INTERVIEWER. And you play other instruments, too?

DOUGLAS. Well, yes I do. See, early on I had this kind of passion for learning musical instruments. I remember when I was ten years old my second brother came along with a guitar. And I'd pick up his guitar from time to time and try to learn things on it. Then I got my own guitar. Then my third brother, as I said, got interested in the french horn, so I started picking up his horn and playing with it. Then when I was in high school I played the french horn in the band.

INTERVIEWER. Oh my gosh, so there you were, piano . . . guitar . . . french horn . . . .

DOUGLAS. Then it started to snowball. I saw a clarinet at a garage sale so I picked it up — five bucks [dollars] — went home and pretty soon I was making music on it. Then, about the same time, I saw a trombone and a trumpet in a pawn shop and had to have them. Again, taught myself the little I knew. I'd go to music stores and buy the beginners' books, and they tell you what to do, how to get started.

INTERVIEWER. And I suppose the brass instruments are similar in some ways, aren't they?

DOUGLAS. Exactly, so once I knew how to play one of them, I had a good start on the others. Then one of my brothers brought home a mandolin, and I discovered one of the violins in the closet, and before I knew it, I had a banjo and a flute.

INTERVIEWER. Oh my gosh, stop. You're making me dizzy. It would be like learning French, then Spanish or Italian, then starting with Russian, and Chinese and Arabic . . . I just . . . boggles . . . .

DOUGLAS. It was crazy. But that was my passion, like I said.

INTERVIEWER. Well, then after high school did you go on to study music in a college or not?

DOUGLAS. Well, I did, for a while, but I'm what I guess you call a college drop-out. I left college to, you know, to get on with life. I got my first job — musical job that is — that summer, in a Mexican restaurant.

INTERVIEWER. In Mexico?

DOUGLAS. No, in Virginia. I had moved to Virginia Beach; that's where one of my brothers was living. I packed all my instruments and sent them out from California to Virginia on a Greyhound bus, and I rode my motorcycle across the country. It took seven long days. And as it turned out, my brother and I got this job — part time, Thursday and Sunday nights — playing music in this Mexican restaurant. I played the flute, and he played the guitar. We'd play a lot of Spanish music. We didn't make much money, but we got some pretty good tips. Stayed out there about two years and then went back to California and worked in restaurants, first as a waiter, then later as a cook . . . that's where my cooking got started.

INTERVIEWER. Well, so then at that point you pretty much gave up on your music.

DOUGLAS. Well, at that point, cooking was how I made my living, and music was my hobby. Then I moved to Aspen, Colorado — you know the famous ski resort — and I had a cooking job again. That's where I met Jane, my wife, and that's where my music began to take off. I started writing songs, and I'd play them for friends, sitting around in front of the fireplace after work. Then I started performing for après ski in one of the lounges, and I had a solid job from four to six every day.

INTERVIEWER. And you did that in addition to your cooking?

DOUGLAS. Yeah, I was cooking the breakfast and lunch shift and doing my gig. I found that the more I played and sang, the more comfortable I got with it and the better I got with it. And I kept that up there in Aspen for four years — that was 1984. That's when I decided to go for it. Not just play around with music but to make that the central thing — make my living with it. Then Jane and I decided to get married, and we moved here to New Hampshire.

INTERVIEWER. And so you had decided to make your living then with music and have cooking as your hobby?

DOUGLAS. Exactly. Can I get you another Dutch baby?

INTERVIEWER. Yes, but I do want to hear another one of your songs.

DOUGLAS. Sure, but later. Now eat. Would you like some coffee?

INTERVIEWER. Please. I'd come to your restaurant any day if you were the cook. Especially with these Dutch babies. Compliments to the chef.

DOUGLAS. Well, thank you.

Questions

The general comprehension questions which are given in the student's book on page 44 should be discussed after the first listening to the interview.

Vocabulary in Context ✹ 2

Tape: Part Two — Listening exercise

Listen to this recording and write down the word or phrase you hear. You will hear the word or phrase twice. Then, listen to two sentences in which that word or phrase is used. The second sentence is taken from the conversation you've just heard. Next, write down what you think that word or phrase means. Make an intelligent guess, using context clues.

1. **to stick with   to stick with**
   Example: I didn't like my job, but I decided I should stick with it, and I did. In fact, I'm still working there.
   From the tape: My oldest brother studied the violin, but he didn't stick with it.

2. **to be cut out for   to be cut out for**
   Example: Teaching is interesting work, but I don't think I'm cut out for it. I just don't have enough patience.
   From the tape: . . . you know, the routine of having to practice. He wasn't cut out for that.

3. **From early on   from early on**
   Example: From early on my son wanted to be a musician. In fact I think he made that decision the very first time he played a guitar when he was five years old.
   From the tape: You see, from early on I had this kind of like passion for learning musical instruments.

4. **to get on with   to get on with**
   Example: I think we have played long enough. Now, let's get on with our work.
   From the tape: I left college to, you know, to get on with my life.

5. **to take off   to take off**
   Example: I'm flying to New York City this afternoon. My flight takes off at three o'clock.
   From the tape: . . . that's where my music began to take off.

6. **to make a living   to make a living**
   Example: I make my living as an engineer. My wife makes hers as a teacher.
   From the tape: Not just play around with music but to make that the central thing — make my living with it.

51

Additional vocabulary

7. **to turn out**   to turn out
   Example: And how did the dinner turn out? Badly. Nobody liked the food.
   From the tape: ... And as it turned out, my brother and I got this job.

8. **[to] drop out**   [to] drop out
   Example: Then my friend moved to Florida and I never saw him again. He just dropped out of my life.
   From the tape: Well, I did, for a while, but I'm what I guess you call a college drop-out.

9. **to go for it**   to go for it
   Example: First, I thought that it was too much to apply for the scholarship. But then, I changed my mind and decided to go for it.
   From the tape: That was in 1984. That's when I decided I'd go for it.

Definitions of vocabulary in context

1. to continue doing something that is not very easy
2. to be appropriate for or suitable for
3. from a young age, in this case, probably about four or five years old
4. to begin or continue doing something
5. to leave the ground; to rise, ascend; to begin to be successful
6. to earn enough money to live on
7. to be the final result
8. to leave, to disappear from, to quit
9. to make a big effort to do something

The Interview 1

Tape: Part One, again — The second listening

Rewind the tape and listen to the interview again. Then answer the following questions and do the reconstruction exercise.

Detailed Questions

These detailed comprehension questions may be asked after the second listening to the interview. They do not appear in the student's book.

1. Douglas speaks about cooks and folk singers. What does he say?
2. What does he say about waiters and actors?
3. What was his father's relationship to music?
4. What was his mother's relationship to music? Why didn't she do very much with music?
5. What do you remember about the size of Doug's family?
6. What did you learn about the place of music in Douglas' family?
7. Explain how Douglas learned to play musical instruments.
8. What was his passion?
9. Describe Doug's experience in college. Why did he leave college?
10. He worked in a Mexican restaurant. Where was it? What did he do there?
11. When he went back to California, he says that "music was my hobby." What does he mean?
12. What were his musical performances in Aspen, Colorado?
13. What else happened in Aspen?
14. What was the big decision that he made in Aspen?

Reconstruction

The exercise which is given in the student's book on page 45 should be done after the second listening to the interview.

The Interview continues 3

Lesson five continues with the third part of the taped material. This is a continuation of the interview with Douglas in his kitchen. After this part of the interview, Douglas sings his song, "California." Listen to the dialogue and then listen to the song, trying to understand it without looking at the words. Then answer the questions in your book.

INTERVIEWER. Douglas, you promised that you'd sing your song called "California" for me. But before you sing it, would you tell me something about how you compose your songs. You do write both the words and the music for your songs, don't you?

DOUGLAS. Yes.

INTERVIEWER. Well, how does it work? How does it happen? How do you do it?

DOUGLAS. Well, sometimes it can be very easy. And other times it's kind of difficult. When I'm writing I always try to keep my mind wide open for everything that comes along. I try not to censor anything that comes to my mind. In a way, that is, the words and the music just flow naturally, and they come together. That's when things are going well. That was true, for example, with "Fill My Thirst." The whole thing took just about a half an hour. I was sitting at this table, and it just started coming to me.

53

INTERVIEWER. . . . .in half an hour, you did the whole thing?

DOUGLAS. Well, other songs take a lot longer. "You Get What's Coming" took me a long time to write. I got the first part of it easily, and it was just a story that was unfolding in my imagination. There again, I didn't want to censor it so I said to myself, "O.K., then what happened?" So, I'm listening in my head and I'm trying to hear what's the next line that comes, and I get the next line. Then there's my song "California." I was sitting there in Telluride, Colorado, where Jane and I were living for six months before we moved here to New Hampshire. I was missing California, you know that's my home. That's where I was born and where I grew up. I was missing it. So I sat down and just began to think about California. I began playing with my guitar. The song is really about my family history . . . how my great-grandfather went to California . . . to San Francisco. He had left Portland, Maine, to go to California, and he sailed tug boats on the San Francisco Bay. Oakland was a big port town . . . still is but it's changed a lot. He was my great-grandfather. My great-grandmother was actually from Bunker Hill in Boston. She had been orphaned at age five and went to live in a convent. And that's where she lived as a child. Then, she married an Irishman, had eighteen or nineteen children, I don't remember which. But he was a ladies' man, and he ran around a lot, and he gambled, and he drank a lot, and she was so disgusted that she finally divorced him.

INTERVIEWER. She divorced him after nineteen children?

DOUGLAS. Yeah, after nineteen children, and, of course, that was just not done in those days. You didn't get a divorce. But she did, and then she met my great-grandfather there in San Francisco and married him. So he's really my great-grandfather, and he's the one I mention in the song, "California." Then, she had one more child. That was my grandmother.

INTERVIEWER. But isn't that amazing. Your grandmother was your great-grandmother's twentieth child, is that right? And the last. So you have a real California history, going way back, don't you?

DOUGLAS. Yeah, my mother and my father were both born in San Francisco. Beautiful San Francisco.

INTERVIEWER. Well, but the California you sing about in the song . . . . I've heard it now several times . . . .

DOUGLAS. Oh, the California I sing about in the song is a very changed California. For one thing, no trees basically. In the Bay area, for instance, they cut down all the trees then just planted a few back in around the homes. And that kind of thing. And where they took fields that were wild oats and oak trees, they're all gone. The population in the area has grown from maybe about a million people to about twelve million people and that's just in about fifteen years. And not just that, but the people who move into California think they have to look and act just a little bit crazy because it is California.

INTERVIEWER. Now, in that California song you say — am I right? I mean, I've heard it many times — I think you say, "They came for their fortune and they robbed you of yours." What do you mean by that?

DOUGLAS. Yeah, they came to find their fortune, and they robbed California of its fortune — that is, the absolutely breathtaking, beautiful scenery which existed. And it's still there in places, but it's not the same. See, in my mind I can see that beautiful place before the white man came there, before San Francisco was built. It was just those beautiful hills before the white man came there, now I see how that has all changed and spoiled.

INTERVIEWER. I guess it isn't a very happy song.

DOUGLAS. A sad song. But it's not a negative song.

INTERVIEWER. "California," I think you write, "You'll always be my home, but you may never be my home again." Is that right? Is that what you . . . ? I hope you'll explain that to me sometime. I don't quite understand it. But now, anyway . . . Play the tape for me, will you?

DOUGLAS. Sure.

Questions

The discussion questions given in the student's book at the top of page 46 should be used after listening to the continuation of the interview and the song "California."

California

I think I knew you early on
Before the chords of white-man's song
Rang heavy in your hills.
By the hundreds in those days
They came to live in other ways
To see their dreams fulfilled.

My great-grandaddy came to stay,
Ran tugs on San Francisco Bay,
Took Oakland as his home.
He worked away his life to give
The children of his wife a place
To settle down and live.

    California, my heart is warm for you.
    You'll always be my home,
    But you may never be my home again.

Born in Redwood before dawn
My life with you was just a song
I thought would never end.
But then by millions people came;
The gold was now a different game,
But people played to win.

    California, my heart is warm for you.
    You'll always be my home,
    But you may never be my home again.

How I miss your silver bay,
I long to feel the ocean spray.
Oh, I love to see the Golden Gate at sunset,
But far too many feel your breeze.
They know you now and they love your trees.
I just can't be alone with you,
But I won't forget.

    California, my heart is warm for you.
    You'll always be my home,
    But you may never be my home again.

O California,
They came for their fortunes,
And they robbed you of yours.

    I said, California, my heart is warm for you.
    You'll always be my home,
    But you may never be my home again.

The Interview concludes 4

The following is the conclusion of the interview with Douglas Clegg. After listening to it, answer the questions in your book.

INTERVIEWER. One more thing I want to know, and I hope you'll excuse my question, but can you make a living as a folk singer in New England?

DOUGLAS. Well, yeah, you have to be careful, because you can't go crazy buying things, and I don't drive an expensive car and those kinds of things. You're not going to be rich.

INTERVIEWER. Well, how do you do it?

DOUGLAS. Well, you have to work hard. You have to keep plugging away, making your contacts, promoting yourself. You've got to work a lot of jobs. It takes a lot of work. .

INTERVIEWER. And you've got to keep hauling that equipment, right?

DOUGLAS. Sure, that's work, but, you know, it takes more energy to perform than it does to load the equipment. It's work to perform. It's so demanding. You're acting in a sense because you're performing and you're on stage. You may have a headache or worse, but you can't convey you have a headache. You have to put on a happy face, and you've got to produce.

INTERVIEWER. Well, and I'm sure you've set for yourself a certain high standard of performance. And to be satisfied, you have to meet that standard which you have set for yourself. And that takes concentration. And there are all those distractions ... people out there ....

DOUGLAS. And even if you've sung the song a thousand times, you are still thinking and concentrating and creating. And for the audience, it has to look like it's easy. But, you've put so much time into perfecting it that it's almost easy to be good. Because it is true that the more times you've played that piece and worked at it, the better it gets. And that's also part of the fun and pleasure of all this. That's exciting to get that music really sounding good.

INTERVIEWER. And I suppose that part of the work is figuring out your audience because I imagine that audiences are very different from each other.

DOUGLAS. Right. You never know who's going to be there listening. And if you're playing in a bar or a club, you don't know if they're going to be listening or talking to their friends and drinking. Of course, if it's a concert, that's different. They've come to listen. So you have to be flexible, and you have to tune in to your audience and cater to them. You've got to figure out what music is going to appeal to them and then work with that. You can see, that's part of the work, but that's part of the interesting creative side of being a folk singer.

INTERVIEWER. Are there other pleasures too?

DOUGLAS. Well, I work for myself. I make my own schedule. A lot of freedom. One of the biggest plusses for me is that this does not have a finite goal ... the sky's the limit. There's no telling how far I may get with this. Now, I've released a record. That's a big step, you know. There are many possibilities to get better known. To get larger audiences. A lot of room for expansion. A lot of room to grow.

INTERVIEWER. Well, do you have to have large audiences, larger audiences? Can't you continue to grow and not have larger audiences?

DOUGLAS. Well, that's possible I suppose. But, the two things, growth and the larger audiences, seem to go hand in hand. As you develop musically, you're going to wind up with bigger and more attentive audiences. Of course, it also depends on your ability to entertain. You may be an awfully good musician, but you also have to be able to entertain. So you have to develop both as a musician and an entertainer. See what I mean?

INTERVIEWER. Well, so you have to be good, but you also have to be tuned in to your audience, is that what you're saying?

DOUGLAS. Exactly, like an actor in the theater, like a haircutter with his client.

INTERVIEWER. Like a teacher ....
DOUGLAS. Like a waiter with his table ....
INTERVIEWER. Like ....
DOUGLAS. Like the North Wind blowing down the prairie.
INTERVIEWER. And if you're tuned in, you can get what's coming!
DOUGLAS. Hey, that's the title of a song I wrote.
INTERVIEWER. Yes!
DOUGLAS. "You Get What's Coming."
INTERVIEWER. You get what's coming!

Questions

The discussion questions given in the student's book at the bottom of page 46 should be used after listening to the conclusion of the interview.

The Interactive Listening  5

Tape: Part One — The final song

You are about to hear Douglas sing another of his songs. First listen to the song and try to understand its meaning. This time the words to the song are given in your student's book on page 48, but some of the words have been left out. Listen to the song again and fill in the missing words. Then, answer the questions which follow the song.

Answers to the interactive listening exercise

feet/head	slaves	playing
just	tales/fortunes	sound
overtime	trade	
waste	lucky	private/railroad
behind		time of day
	sound	sipped
		brain
understand		
man	low	
sand	pool/cool	
	turned	
sound	"Gold!"	
	deep/below	

The Projects

A choice of communicative activities

The projects are designed to be done concurrently with the listening work. The explanations for the projects start on page 49 of the student's book.

57

Lesson Six

Helen Chandler

Volunteer

Note to the teacher or tutor:

Lesson six is again atypical in format. There is no dialogue. During the interview the students are asked to write their own dialogue based on what they have learned listening to the interview. The students may then read their dialogues to the class or tape them on audio or video cassettes. (For an explanation of techniques using taping, see Technology Assisted Teaching Techniques *from Pro Lingua Associates.)*

In the interactive listening exercise there are no absolutely correct or incorrect answers since the match of volunteer job to volunteer is made by each student, but during discussion students should be asked to justify the choices they have made.

Introductory Reading ⚹

This reading, which is given in the student's book on page 51, should be discussed as a prelistening exercise.

58

Work Related Vocabulary — with definitions

1. a **volunteer**: a person who performs or gives his services of his/her own free will
2. **publicity**: information concerning a person, group, event, or product that is brought to public notice through the media or other means
3. **funding**: setting aside an amount of money for a specific purpose
4. **advertising**: to make known the qualities or advantages of a product or business so as to increase sales
5. a **directory**: a book listing names, addresses, or other data about a specific group
6. **federal agencies**: central government departments that have specific jobs; for example, HUD is an agency in Washington that is concerned with housing.
7. a **fire hazard**: anything that may cause a fire accidentally, such as bad electrical wiring, or something that may create more danger if there is a fire, such as a door that won't open
8. an **apartment superintendent**: the person hired to take care of the apartment building
9. **garbage and trash**: food wastes from a kitchen, worthless or discarded materials
10. **rent control**: a system of laws that limits the amount of rent a landlord can get from a tenant.
11. **social welfare**: a means of helping the poor in our society, organized by government
12. a **welfare check**: a payment of welfare money
13. an **addiction**: a state of being unable to control one's use of drugs, alcohol, gambling, food, etc.
14. an **abortion**: the ending of a pregnancy before the fetus is capable of surviving
15. **child abuse**: hurting or injuring a child; treating a child harmfully
16. **consumer problem**: A consumer is a buyer and user of products. If a consumer has a problem with a product he/she has bought, it is a consumer problem.

Additional vocabulary

1. a **widow**: a woman whose husband has died
2. **luxury**: something that leads to great physical comfort or sumptuous living
3. a **saga**: a very long narrative or story
4. **defective**: not in proper working condition; flawed.
5. **reputable**: having a good reputation; known to be good.
6. a **flat tire**: a deflated tire

The Interview ✳ 1

Tape: Part One — The first listening

Lesson Six of People at Work begins with an interview with volunteer, Helen Chandler. Before listening, review the work related vocabulary in your book on page 52. You will listen to the interview at least twice. After the first listening, answer the questions in your book and then do the vocabulary in context exercise, using both your book and this tape. When you have finished the vocabulary in context, rewind and listen to the interview with Helen again.

The interview takes place at Helen's desk at radio station WBZ's Call for Action office. Now, Helen Chandler, volunteer.

INTERVIEWER. Helen, first, I have to ask you a kind of a silly question. Is this a real job? I mean do you get paid for it?

HELEN. A real job? Of course it's a real job. But, no, I don't get paid for it. You see, I'm a volunteer here.

INTERVIEWER. O.K., and volunteers don't get paid, here.

HELEN. That's right. The story is that I'm a widow ... my husband died several years ago. And all those years of our marriage I was what was called back then a "housewife."

INTERVIEWER. Housewife!

HELEN. You remember housewives?

INTERVIEWER. Oh, sure I do.

HELEN. Well, I was one of those housewives who were happy to be taking care of the house, cooking, cleaning, shopping, looking after my husband, and busily raising four children.

INTERVIEWER. Well, there aren't many left, are there, in this country ... housewives, I mean. What family has the luxury now of ... ?

HELEN. Oh yes ... Most married women do work now. For one thing, in today's economy most families have to have those two incomes.

INTERVIEWER. But, don't you think, though, that a lot of married women today, maybe even most of them, want to work?

HELEN. I think that's probably true. But my story is that I had always been a housewife, and when my husband died he left me some money — not all that much — but I didn't really have to work. I could do exactly what I wanted to do, something I thought was valuable and important. And that's why I'm here at the Call for Action office at WBZ.

INTERVIEWER. I guess I'm surprised to see that your office here at BZ ... I mean, first I'm surprised that it's here, but then I don't quite understand why ...

HELEN. Oh, the fact of the matter is that every radio station is required by law to give a certain amount of free service to its listeners, so WBZ gives us our office, our telephones, publicity, funding, and advertising. All free. And we volunteers do the rest. It's really a great arrangement for us. I think for them, too. Mutually beneficial.

INTERVIEWER. And for you, of course, WBZ has a lot of power in the community — a lot of clout, I'm sure. But, I'm a little surprised to see how small your office is. Just this one small room here?

HELEN. Oh, there's one other small room right behind that curtain. And our only equipment is these five telephones and this directory.

INTERVIEWER. Oh it's huge, isn't it! What is it?

HELEN. There are hundreds and hundreds of pages, with descriptions of all the organizations in Boston as well as over 600 city, state, and federal agencies. Take a look ...

INTERVIEWER. (A whistle) ... Huge ... so then you sit here and answer the phone? Is that it?

HELEN. Well, that's the beginning. I come in for two hours, twice a week, and answer the phone and what I do is ... well, whenever people call I try to connect them with the organization or agency or person ... whatever ... who can help them find an answer to their question or problem. Sometimes we do some phoning ourselves to speed up the process.

INTERVIEWER. Could you give me an idea how that works.

HELEN. Sure. But you wouldn't believe the incredible variety of crazy situations we hear about. Oh now, where to start. Well, just this morning — it all started two days ago — a woman called; she was frantic. It seems that she lives in a large apartment building, and she lives on the twenty-third floor. The building has three elevators. Well, for two weeks, only one of the elevators had been running, and two days ago the third one went kapooey. Picture this if you can. Here is this woman, living on the twenty-third floor. She comes back from shopping with her small baby and three huge bags of groceries ....

INTERVIEWER. . . and she has to walk up twenty-three flights of stairs because there's no elevator. So she complained, I suppose. And she called you here.

HELEN. Well, but first you see, she had gone to the apartment superintendent three times to complain; she and others. Nothing happened for five days. So then she called city hall to complain. Again, nothing. That's when she got the idea to call us here at WBZ Call for Action two days ago. I'd never heard anything quite like this before, so I talked it over with Ruby Eldrige — she's the volunteer over there at phone number three. Ruby had the bright idea to call the fire department. I would never have thought of it. You see if an elevator isn't working there is a ... can you guess?

INTERVIEWER. .... hum. What? A fire hazard?

HELEN. Yes, a fire hazard.

INTERVIEWER. Of course. But what a brilliant idea.

HELEN. And that's what I did. Some fireman answered the phone and connected me to the fire chief and I quietly but firmly said this is WBZ Call For Action. I could just see him sit up straight when I said, "Call For Action." I told him the whole saga, and he agreed that something needed to be done immediately. So he calls the apartment superintendent, demands that the elevator be repaired. One hour later, all three elevators were working. The woman just called me back to tell me the good news. I'm delighted, of course; I love getting action like that.

INTERVIEWER. Wow. What an amazing story. Clout! You people really do have clout, don't you?

HELEN. Well, that's a good word for it.

INTERVIEWER. What about housing problems? Do you get a lot of calls about housing problems?

HELEN. Oh, I could tell you hundreds of stories like that one: people angry about neighbors in their apartment building who leave garbage and trash in the hallway; fights with landlord; disputes over rent control ... that sort of thing.

INTERVIEWER. Well, what other kinds of calls do you get?

HELEN. Well, I guess we get a lot of what you might call "social welfare" questions and problems. All kinds of things. Well, for example, a divorced woman will call because her welfare check is late and her family is hungry. And then there are different kinds of addictions: a person will call who has an alcohol or drug or a smoking addiction and wants to do something about it. People ask abortion questions, all sorts of family problems, child abuse, that sort of thing.

INTERVIEWER. What about "consumer" problems?

HELEN. Oh, and of course, consumer problems. We get lots and lots of those calls.

INTERVIEWER. Well, I think I've got one myself.

HELEN. A consumer problem?

INTERVIEWER. Um hm.

HELEN. Well, tell me about it.

INTERVIEWER. Well, it's about a refrigerator I bought eight days ago.

HELEN. It's defective?

INTERVIEWER. Well, I don't know. It hasn't been delivered yet.

HELEN. Hasn't been delivered after eight days?

INTERVIEWER. No. I bought this refrigerator from a good, reputable downtown Boston store. Nice refrigerator. I told them I needed it the next day, and they said, "Hey, sure, we can deliver it tomorrow. No problem!" That was on Tuesday. Last Friday, three days later, I still didn't have it. So I called. I was really quite angry. I asked why they hadn't delivered the refrigerator. This secretary says, "Oh, I'm very sorry, but our delivery truck has two flat tires, but we're hoping we can deliver sometime tomorrow."

61

HELEN. You still don't have your refrigerator.

INTERVIEWER. Right. Any suggestions?

HELEN. Yes, I'm going to get on the phone. Tell me the name of the store.

INTERVIEWER. Hey, hey wait, Helen. Now I see why you're so good at this job. You just get on that phone, and you let 'em have it.

HELEN. That's it ... it's the best way.

INTERVIEWER. Well, first, let me ask the students something. Students, if you were Helen, what would you say. Take some time now, write down your ideas of Helen's phone call about my refrigerator. Then read it out loud to your class or record it.

HELEN. Ed, I'm waiting.

INTERVIEWER. Well, O.K. O.K. The store is called Boston Home Appliances, and I ....

Questions

The general comprehension questions which are given in the student's book on page 53 should be discussed after the first listening to the interview.

Vocabulary in Context 2

Tape: Part Two — Listening exercise

Listen to the recording and write down the word or phrase you hear. You will hear the word or phrase twice. Then, listen to two sentences in which that word or phrase is used. The second sentence is taken from the interview you have just heard. Next, write down what you think that word or phrase means, in your book. Make an intelligent guess, using the context clues.

1. **mutually beneficial**   **mutually beneficial**
   Example: It is mutually beneficial for us to study the test together. You can teach me what you know, and I can teach you what I know.
   From the tape: It's a really great arrangement for us ... I think for them, too. Mutually beneficial.

2. **incredible**   **incredible**
   Example: The weather this winter has been incredible. It has been warm and sunny every day.
   From the tape: You wouldn't believe the incredible variety of situations we hear about.

3. **frantic**   **frantic**
   Example: When I couldn't find the check for $2,000, I was frantic, and I began to tear the house apart looking for it.
   From the tape: It all started two days ago. A woman called. She was frantic!

4. **fire hazard**   **fire hazard**
   Example: If you keep matches where small children can find them, those matches are a fire hazard.
   From the tape:
   HELEN. You see, if an elevator isn't working there is a — can you guess?
   INTERVIEWER. hmm ... a fire hazard?
   HELEN. Yes, a fire hazard.

5. **clout**   **clout**
   Example: John likes being the president of our organization because he thinks the president has a lot of clout.
   From the tape: The station has a lot of power in this community — a lot of clout, I'm sure.

Definitions of vocabulary in context

1. advantageous to both people
2. unbelievable
3. emotionally distraught from fear, pain or worry; desperate
4. something which is dangerous because it could cause a fire.
5. power, prestige or influence, such as political clout

The Interview ✳ 1

Tape: Part One, again — The second listening

Rewind the tape and listen to the interview again. Then answer the following questions and do the reconstruction exercise.

Detailed Questions

These detailed comprehension questions may be asked after the second listening to the interview. They do not appear in the student's book.

1. Helen sits at a phone. What does she do there?
2. What are some of the things that people call Helen about?
3. Why is Call For Action at station WBZ?
4. What services does WBZ give to Call For Action?
5. The interviewer says that Call For Action has a lot of "clout." What does he mean?
6. According to Helen, it is "mutually beneficial" for WBZ and Call For Action to work together. Why?
7. Describe the problem of the woman who had to use the stairway.
8. Explain why Helen called the fire department.
9. Give details about the interviewer and the refrigerator he ordered.
10. Do you think Helen enjoys this work? Why or why not?
11. What do we learn about the interviewer?

Reconstruction

The exercise which is given in the student's book on page 54 should be done after the second listening to the interview.

The Dialogue — not on the tape

Helen's phone call to Boston Home Appliances.

The students write and, perhaps, record their own dialogues.

Topics for discussion or writing

The discussion topics are given in the student's book on page 55.

The Interactive Listening 4

Tape: Part Four — Finding jobs for willing volunteers

In this exercise you will help find work for willing volunteers to do. In your student's book on page 56 is a list of descriptions of volunteer jobs for which workers are needed. Read over the list carefully. Next listen to seven people on the tape. Each of them explains who they are, and why they want to volunteer. Your job is to match the volunteers with the volunteer jobs which need doing and then to write your suggestions down on the form which follows the job descriptions in your book.

Volunteer Number 1: My name is Bill. I was a salesmen for a publishing company. I was involved in an auto accident several years ago and have had several operations since then. Although I am in a wheel-chair, I am anxious to do something to fill up my time, to help other people, and just to get myself out of the house.

Volunteer Number 2: My name is Joe. Last year I retired from the Police Force. Then, after my wife and I took a vacation in Hawaii, I spent a lot of time doing projects around the house — little projects I had never had time for. Now, time is hanging heavily on my hands, and I would like to do something that would help other people and make me feel useful again

Volunteer Number 3: I think you recognize my voice, don't you? Anyway, I have a daughter who is fourteen years old, and she has no plans for the summer, and she tells me that she would like to volunteer her services somewhere. Well, she loves nature, and if she could do volunteer work in a park, I know she'd be very happy.

Volunteer Number 4: I'm a senior at the university. I'm still not sure of what I'm going to do when I finish school. This year I am only taking three courses, and I'd like to try something that might lead to a future career.

Volunteer Number 5: I am recently divorced. My children are in college. Although I work three days a week, I have too much time on my hands, and I'm sure I could be useful somewhere.

Volunteer Number 6: I was a teacher before I got married. Right now I am a housewife with two little kids. I love them, but they drive me crazy sometimes, and I'd love to get away from them one morning a week, get dressed up, and go out into the world. But I'd also like to do something useful.

Volunteer Number 7: I am a retired accountant. For the past fifty years I have worked ten to twelve hours a day. What can I do now so that I don't go crazy and drive my wife crazy as well?

Volunteer Number 8 is you: Describe yourself and choose one of the fifteen volunteer jobs for yourself.

The Projects

A *choice of communicative activities*

The projects are designed to be done concurrently with the listening work. The explanations for the projects start on page 58 of the student's book.

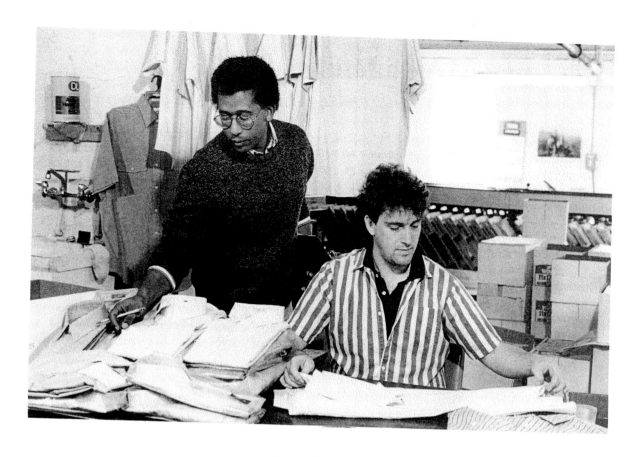

Lesson Seven

Sam Adams
Industrial Engineer

Note to the teacher or tutor:

The seventh lesson is atypical in that the interview is interrupted and the students are asked on tape to give some suggestions. Then, after the vocabulary in context exercise and the reconstruction work, but before the dialogue, the interview is resumed with a short listening section in which Sam talks about the suggestions he made. The students are then asked to compare their suggestions with Sam's before going on to the dialogue. This sequence may be a bit confusing to your students, but following written and aural instructions is "all part of the game" — in other words, it's good practice. Monitor their work, but let them figure out what to do if they can.

At the very end of this lesson, there is part of a letter written by Sam. If any students have assumed that Sam with his bachelor's degree must have been very knowledgable about his field, this letter may change their point of view. The letter is given here in your teacher's book so that you can spring it on your students when the time is right. Feel free to photocopy it for handouts.

The project which asks the students to analyze help wanted ads is a useful one. Often the vocabulary of these ads is unknown to the students, and even if it is known, the elliptical style is confusing and the ads are difficult to interpret.

Introductory Reading ✌

This reading, which is given in the student's book on page 61, should be discussed as a prelistening exercise.

66

Work Related Vocabulary — with definitions

1. an **efficiency expert**: a person who studies the methods and procedures of a factory or business in order to improve its production
2. a **payroll**: a list of persons in a business or organization who receive pay, with the amount of pay they receive
3. a **union**: an organization of workers who are united for their mutual benefit. They often have a pay increase and or improved working conditions as a common goal.
4. **non-union**: refers to workers who are not members of a workers' union.
5. **labor**: a collective noun referring to the work force; people who work, often as distinguished from those who manage who are called the management
6. a **short-term basis**: a temporary, not permanent situation. Here, Sam was hired to consult for just a short amount of time.
7. a **consultant**: a person hired to give advice
8. **quality control**: a system for inspecting and controlling the quality of products
9. a **product**: that which is produced or made by work
10. to **go on strike**: to refuse to work until certain demands are met by management
11. an **assembly line**: the place where factory products are put together (assembled) by the workers, each repeating his/her job many times.
12. **work flow**: the movement of work from worker to worker — slow or fast, steady or unsteady, etc.
13. a **minimum wage**: the lowest amount of money — established by law or by a labor union — which employers can pay for those who work for them

Additional vocabulary

1. a **slob**: a messy (not neat and tidy) person
2. **hammers, saws, nails**: the basic tools used in carpentry
3. **kitchen utensils**: knives, forks, spoons and the other basic instruments used in a kitchen
4. **monotony**: a sameness in routine which is tiring and boring
5. **boredom**: the condition of having no interest; being bored

The Interview ✳ 1

Tape: Part One — The first listening

Lesson Seven begins with an interview with industrial engineer, Sam Adams. Before listening, review the work related vocabulary in your book on page 62. You will listen to the interview at least twice. After the first listening, answer the questions in your book and then do the vocabulary in context exercise, using both your book and this tape. When you have finished the vocabulary in context, rewind and listen to the interview with Sam again. Now, Sam Adams, industrial engineer.

SAM. Is the microphone on?

INTERVIEWER. Yes, but just forget about it.

SAM. O.K. I'll try to forget about it. But I want to ask one thing before we start the regular interview. This interview is for some sort of a book, right?

INTERVIEWER. That's right. It's going to be a series of taped interviews of typical working people in the United States, like yourself, and there's a school teacher, and there's a waiter, and there's an intern in a hospital. We have 10 chapters altogether. Actually, it's for international students studying English.

SAM. That gives me an idea. Now, what do you want to know. Shoot.

INTERVIEWER. Well, first of all I'm curious about how you happened to end up as an industrial engineer. I'm curious about what kinds of personal interests and talents lead a person into that field.

SAM. I have to tell you what my mother says about that.

INTERVIEWER. What does she say?

SAM. Well, she claims that I had all the characteristics of an industrial engineer from the time I was very young … yeah, I mean young, seven, eight, nine years old. She tells me that even back then I always liked to have everything very well organized, very neat.

INTERVIEWER. Huh … organized and neat, huh? Are those necessary characteristics of the profession?

SAM. Sure, they help.

INTERVIEWER. Is that the way you remember it?

SAM. Oh yeah, I can remember when I was still in grade school … fourth, fifth grade. I liked to keep all my socks in the … I think it was … the upper left hand drawer of my bureau. My underwear had to be in the upper right drawer; I put shirts and pajamas in the middle drawer, and pants folded neatly in the bottom drawer.

INTERVIEWER. That seems amazing to me. That's impossible to believe. I was so different from that … I'm sure most kids are … Oh, I was a real slob, totally disorganized. It's hard for me to imagine any eight or nine year-old boy wanting to keep things neat and organized like that.

SAM. Well, and that's not all. Starting when I was about nine, I was the efficiency expert for the whole family. Oh, I used to organize my father's tools … hammers, saws, nails … all that stuff … my mother's kitchen utensils … dishes, glasses, silverware, egg beaters, you name it, but the craziest of all, I remember, you won't believe this: I used to organize my sister's boy friends.

INTERVIEWER. Your sister's boy friends! How in the world could you possible organize…

SAM. No, don't ask me. I don't think she's ever forgiven me for what I did those awful days.

INTERVIEWER. So there was a place for everything and everything was always in its proper place.

SAM. Yes, exactly. But I do think those were the beginnings for a career in industrial engineering. And you know, as I think back on it now, I realize that the flip side of being organized and neat was, for me anyway … uuummm … well, that I was very bossy. I ran things. I ran people.

INTERVIEWER. You're saying, if I understand, that it's O.K. for an industrial engineer to be neat and organized, but he shouldn't tell everyone what to do.

SAM. Yeah, and I didn't know that at the time. So let me tell you about my first job experience in the field. I think you'll see what I mean. This was just after I finished my bachelor's degree. I had returned home to my small town in Indiana.

INTERVIEWER. Oh, you're from Indiana!

SAM. Yeah. I didn't have a job yet, and one day I ran into a friend of my father, Mr. Hobbs, downtown. He owns a small shirt factory in town. He was telling me about his factory and about how it had grown so much in just two years. It had grown from a payroll of ten to a payroll of fifty workers. He said, "Oh I've got a great bunch of workers ... it's all non-union and no trouble with labor." But he said he was worried that his factory was getting too big and inefficient, and he asked me if I would come in on a short-term basis as a consultant.

INTERVIEWER. Sounds perfect. Right down your alley. And you didn't have another job at the time.

SAM. Right. So I went out there and looked around and took notes ... .

INTERVIEWER. And you discovered ... ?

SAM. I was amazed. The place was completely disorganized. The strangest thing was that there was no quality control. No one inspected the final product — the finished shirts. Some of the shirts would be put in boxes for shipment missing a button, maybe two buttons, maybe the collar, a sleeve sometimes.

INTERVIEWER. Huh? You're serious?

SAM. There's more. Working conditions. Awful. The tables where the workers sat were very high and uncomfortable. There was a half hour lunch break, but no other breaks during the day. No music, of course, nothing to relieve the monotony and boredom of the job. The walls of the workroom were a dull gray color.

INTERVIEWER. Hey, how can I get a job down there!

SAM. Yeah, really. But there's more. My second day there I noticed an especially absentminded young man in the assembly line. Workers called him Big Jim. His job was to sew on buttons. Well, he was very slow and the shirts were held up at his position. The workers beyond him in the line often had to wait with nothing to do.

INTERVIEWER. Wow. I'd say you had a few things to report back to Mr. Hobbs.

SAM. Yes, as you can see, there were a lot of things to say. I was at the shirt factory for a week. Then I wrote out my report with my recommendations to Mr. Hobbs.

INTERVIEWER. .... and your recommendations?

SAM. Well, in the first place, l suggested that ....

INTERVIEWER. Hold it, hold it, hold it! I have an idea. Let's ask the students what they think you recommended. Now they've heard your observations and reactions, now let's ask them.

SAM. Sure, I like it.

INTERVIEWER. Shall we do it?

SAM. Go for it.

INTERVIEWER. O.K., students. Take a piece of paper and make a list of the recommendations you think Sam will make to Mr. Hobbs. Work with a partner if you want to.

SAM. Let's see what we get ....

Questions

The general comprehension questions which are given in the student's book on page 63 should be discussed after the first listening to the interview.

Vocabulary in context 2

Tape: Part Two — Listening exercise

Listen to this recording and write down the word or phrase you hear. You will hear the word or phrase twice. Then, listen to two sentences in which that word or phrase is used. The second sentence is taken from the conversation you've just heard. Next, write down what you think that word or phrase means. Make an intelligent guess, using the context clues.

1. shoot   **shoot**

   Example: You have some suggestions to make. I'm ready to listen. Shoot!

   From the tape: Now, what do you want to know? Shoot!

2. end up   **end up**

   Example: How did he end up in California? When I knew him, he was living in Tokyo, and he was planning to move to Chicago.

   From the tape: Well, first of all, I'm curious about how you happened to end up as an industrial engineer.

3. absent-minded   **absent-minded**

   Example: Oh, I'm so absent-minded I can't find my glasses or my watch or my keys at least twice a day.

   From the tape: My second day there I noticed an especially absent-minded young man in the assembly line.

4. the flip side   **the flip side**

   Example: Sure, that's a lot of money to pay for a new car. But the flip side is that you won't have constant expenses for repairs.

   From the tape: I realize that the flip side of being organized and neat was for me, anyway, well, that I was also very bossy.

5. bossy   **bossy**

   Example: I don't like to travel places with my brother because he's so bossy: he wants to make all the decisions about where we eat, where we go, everything.

   From the tape: I was very bossy. I ran things; I ran people.

6. to run [things]   **to run [people]**

   Example: Some people tell me that I'm a very bossy person who likes to run everybody I work with — telling them what to do all the time.

   From the tape: I was very bossy. I ran things; I ran people.

Additional vocabulary

7. to run into   **to run into**

   Example: I was surprised. I didn't know she was in town, and then I ran into her at the university.

   From the tape: I didn't have a job yet, and one day I ran into a friend of my father's.

8. **right down your alley**   **right down your alley**

   Example: I think it would be a very good job for John. He is always fixing cars, and being a mechanic in the garage should be right down his alley.

   From the tape: Sounds perfect. Right down your alley.

9. held up   **held up**

   Example: We were held up in traffic for two hours because there had been a bad accident just ahead on the highway.

   From the tape: He was very slow, and the shirts were held up at his position.

Definitions of vocabulary in context

1. Begin! Start talking.
2. to finally become
3. forgetful
4. the other or opposite side, particularly of a phonograph record or coin
5. acting like a boss; telling others what to do
6. to give directions to others; to tell others what to do
7. to meet someone unexpectedly, by surprise
8. very appropriate, suitable
9. delayed

The Interview 1

Tape: Part One, again — The second listening

Rewind the tape and listen to the interview again. Then answer the following questions and do the reconstruction exercise.

Detailed Questions

These detailed comprehension questions may be asked after the second listening to the interview. They do not appear in the student's book.

1. Sammy talks about how organized he was when he was nine years old. He gives some examples. What are they?
2. Sam says he was the efficiency expert for the whole family when he was very young. What examples does he give?
3. He talks about even organizing his sister's boyfriends. How do you suppose he did that?
4. Who was Mr. Hobbs?
5. Why did Mr. Hobbs want Sam to visit his plant?
6. What did Sam suggest to relieve the monotony of the work?
7. Who was Big Jim?
8. Sam thought the factory needed quality control. Why?
9. Sammy spent a week at the shirt factory as an industrial engineering consultant. Now, review all of the observations he made while he was there.

Reconstruction

The exercise which is given in the student's book on page 64 should be done after the second listening to the interview.

The Interview concludes ✳ 1

Tape: Part One — The first listening

The interview with Sam Adams, industrial engineer, continues. Compare your recommendations with Sam's.

INTERVIEWER. By now you have heard Sam tell about his experience at the shirt factory. You have also enumerated the suggestions you think Sam made to Mr. Hobbs for the improvement of the factory. Now, listen to Sam tell about the suggestions that he actually did make to Mr. Hobbs. O.K., Sam, what were your suggestions?

SAM. You want to hear?

INTERVIEWER. Yeah, let's hear.

SAM. O.K., these were my suggestions. Many of them had to do with efficiency. First, I made some suggestions about the working conditions: give the workers fifteen minute coffee breaks in the morning and afternoon ... at least fifteen minutes ... maybe twenty. Get some background music in there to relieve the monotony. Umm ... the walls ... get the walls painted a pleasant, happy color; get rid of that drab grey that puts you to sleep. Next, they've got to redesign the assembly line so that there's a nice smooth work flow which they don't have now. Find a different place for Big Jim, or train him or fire him or something. They can't go on like that. And of course there's the major issue of quality control. There absolutely must be a final inspection of the product. Is everything right, in place, in order? One other big thing. It concerns the pay. They're paying minimum wage out there, and the workers don't get regular raises. So I suggested that management institute a policy of regular pay raises and promotions, based on the quality of work. Also, everyone who works there should have medical insurance. That's a must. They don't have that now. Those were the major things I wrote in my report to Mr. Hobbs. Now, those things don't sound unreasonable, do they?

INTERVIEWER. Sounds reasonable to me!

The Dialogue 3

Tape: Part Three — A conversation between Sam and Jane

Listen to the conversation and then answer the questions in your book.

JANE. Hey, Sam. How's everything?

SAM. Great to see you, Jane.

JANE. I hear you got a new job with Babson Machines.

SAM. Yeah, it's true. I was really lucky. I started about six months ago; they haven't fired me yet. How's the factory?

JANE. Ah, about the same as always.

SAM. You mean shirts are still coming out without collars or buttons?

JANE. Sometimes it's just the collar and buttons without the shirt. The plant isn't famous for its efficiency, you know.

SAM. Well, I heard there are some changes at the factory. Something about music and a coffee break in the afternoons.

JANE. Music? Oh yeah. Yeah, I guess there is. A lot of good it does, though. The machines make so much noise we can't hear it anyway. And the coffee break! They only give us five minutes. If we run at top speed we can just make it to the coffee machine and back to our work table.

SAM. I can't believe this. I understood that Mr. Hobbs was ready to make a lot of big changes down there at the factory.

JANE. Well, a couple of things have changed. We used to have dull gray walls to look at in between operations. A couple of weeks ago, some painter came in and painted a huge picture of a perfect shirt ... with all its buttons, sleeves, *and* the collar. I guess management wanted to remind us of what we're supposed to be producing there. But can you imagine. A shirt! We see enough shirts all day. We don't need to look up from our work and find one painted on the walls.

SAM. You mean that big shirt doesn't motivate all of you to bigger and better production?

JANE. Well, there's lots of pictures that might motivate us to bigger and better production, but a huge painted shirt? No way! Oh, yes, one other change. Remember Big Jim in our algebra class? He used to work on buttons, and he held up half the assembly line. Well, they promoted him from buttons to sleeves, with a raise in pay. Now he sits at the beginning of the line and holds up *everybody*. There's progress for you.

SAM. Ah, yes, progress: one step forward and two steps backward!

Questions

The discussion questions given in the student's book on page 65 should be used after listening to the dialogue.

The Interactive Listening ✳ 1

Tape: Part Four — Three riddles

Industrial engineers are generally intelligent and thoughtful. They are able to look at a problem and find a solution. They must be good listeners. Are you a good listener? Here are three riddles. Listen carefully. Can you solve them? Explain your solutions in writing in your student's book on page 66.

1. Once upon a time there lived a tribe of people who used earrings to indicate their status and availability. In this tribe there were 800 women; half of these wore one earring each to indicate that they were single and available. Of the other half, half wore two earrings to show that they were married and unavailable, and the remaining women wore no earrings to show that their husbands had been killed in war. How many earrings were there in total?

2. A cowboy who had been out on the range for several weeks was feeling the need for a shave and a haircut. He came to a small town where there was one grocery store, three saloons, and two barbershops. He looked in on the first barber who looked unshaven and had a bad, straggly haircut, and then, after taking some refreshment, he walked over and examined the second barber. He was cleanshaven except for a handsome mustache. Not a hair out of place. He was a pleasure to look at. The cowboy turned around and walked back to the first barbershop where he entered and asked for a shave and a haircut. Why did he do this?

3. A man wanted to buy a beautiful bird for his wife's birthday. He entered a pet shop and spied a gorgeous parrot. He asked about the price. "This is a very expensive bird," the petshop owner replied. "He can say every word he hears." Although it was more than he'd planned to spend, the man bought the bird. In a week he was back. "You cheated me," he said. "The bird is beautiful, but he won't say a word." The pet shop owner had not lied. Please explain.

Answers to the interactive listening exercise

1. 800 earrings. Half of the 800 wore one earring = 400
    Half of the half wore 2 earrings (200x2) = 400
    Half of the half wore no earrings = 0

2. He returned to the first barber because it was evident to him that since there were only two barbers, each had cut the other one's hair.

3. The parrot could repeat every word he could hear. Unfortunately, he was deaf.

Final Reading

This is a section of a letter that Sam wrote to a friend. In it he gives the conclusion of his story about his work for Mr. Hobbs. It can be photocopied and handed out to the class as a follow-up reading and the basis for discussion or writing.

So, I learned that my consultation at the shirt factory had gone virtually unheeded.

Well, frankly, I'm not surprised. You see, while working at the Babson Machine Company as an industrial consultant, I took a night class in management engineering at Northwestern University. My company paid the bill. I like that.

Now I have quite a different idea of what it means to be a "consultant." I used to think that the consultant goes into the factory, studies the problems, makes a diagnosis, suggests cures for the problems, and then encourages the management to implement these suggestions.

I now believe that consultation doesn't work successfully that way. In my management engineering course I learned that first and foremost I have to listen. In the shirt factory I should have listened to the management, the two owners. But then, together, we should have listened to the workers themselves. What did **they** think the problems were? What were their suggestions for solutions?

I tried to shove my suggestions down the owners' throats. The suggestions for improvement weren't theirs or the workers. If workers and management are seriously involved in the consultation, change is not only possible, but inevitable.

At any rate, although the experience was painful in many ways, it provided a good lesson for me.

Even though I didn't succeed in this first assignment of mine, Mr. Hobbs was nice enough to give me a check for $100 and a box of shirts. Now I'm thinking of sending the check back to Mr. Hobbs. I'm not sure what to do with the shirts. Four of the five in the box didn't fit anyway, and the fifth one didn't have a right sleeve.

Best wishes,

Sammy

Sammy

The Projects

A choice of communicative activities

The projects are designed to be done concurrently with the listening work. The explanation for the projects start on page 67 of the student's book.

Lesson Eight

Rebecca Kraus
Assistant Dean of Students

Rebecca Kraus has become Dean of Engineering by a circuitous route. Like many of us, she has followed her interests and her opportunities from one position to another. It is why she understands the student who is unsure of the path he is going to follow.

For some students, the most difficult listening section of this lesson is the interactive listening exercise which is designed like a TOEFL listening test. There are eight projects for lesson eight. The first three deal with issues of general interest. The other five concern the academic world where Rebecca is making her career.

Introductory Reading 🌿

This reading, which is given in the student's book on page 75, should be discussed as a prelistening exercise.

Work Related Vocabulary — with definitions

1. **tubes and circuits**: electronic power mechanism or device; electronic wiring or wire patterns and routes.
2. **vacuum tubes**: a glass electron tube enclosing a vacuum for temperature insulation
3. **[computer] software**: computer disks containing computer programs, procedures, rules, and/or data pertaining to the operation of a computer system
4. **[computer] hardware**: the electronic and mechanical devices that comprise a computer system — i.e., personal computer, printer, keyboard, monitor
5. **systems engineering**: Engineers who do systems engineering design computers to implement and study systems that will help industry and organizations work efficiently.
6. **digital processing**: the processing or handling of numbers as expressed in digits (as in the binary system)
7. **a systems analyst**: one who analyzes large complicated systems, usually in business, industry, or government
8. **civil engineering**: engineering concerned with the design and construction of public works
9. **contraction theories**: theories studied by civil enginers which are concerned with materials shrinking or expanding because of temperature, etc.
10. **stress**: a force that puts pressure on a body
11. **reinforced concrete**: concrete (a manmade building material resembling rock) which is strengthened with metal rods.
12. **elasticity**: the capability of a device or mechanism to change in size or shape and return to its original size or shape; adaptability, springiness, resilience
13. **a teaching assistant**: a graduate student, usually getting the most advanced degree, who helps a senior professor
14. **tuition**: the cost, price, or payment for instruction and/or attending school
15. **curriculum work**: the courses offered or taken at college or educational institutions; organized or planned school activities
16. **transfer students**: students entering a college or school from another college or school, usually at the same college year or level of instruction

Additional vocabulary

1. **a rumbling sound**: a low-frequency heavy, continuous reverberating noise
2. **music conservatory**: a music school, usually for advanced students, specializing in technical instruction and practical performance
3. **to plunge into**: to absorb oneself completely, to engage deeply, to immerse oneself (in a book), to dive or jump into headfirst, to go forward recklessly
4. **apoplectic**: astonished, astounded, very upset
5. **a loony bin**: an insane asylum; madhouse; place for the insane (rude terms); mental institutions; mental hospital
6. **absurd**: foolish; ridiculous
7. **conceited**: egotistical; vain
8. **obstinate**: stubborn; willful
9. **to delve into**: dig into; seek out information; investigate

The Interview ✳ 1

Tape: Part One — The first listening

Lesson Eight of People at Work begins with an interview with Dean Rebecca Kraus. Before listening, review the work related vocabulary in your book. You will listen to the interview at least twice. After the first listening, answer the questions in your book and then do the vocabulary in context exercise, using both your book and this tape. When you have finished the vocabulary in context, rewind and listen to the interview with Rebecca again. We are in Dean Kraus's office at the university for this interview. It is a comfortable office where the Dean can talk privately with students when she needs to. The only hint of her background and interests are the beautiful framed engineering plans for the Brooklyn Bridge on one wall and an engraved portrait of Wolfgang Amadeus Mozart on another. Now, Assistant Dean of Students, Rebecca Kraus.

INTERVIEWER. You what?

REBECCA. I got into engineering because of my interest in music.

INTERVIEWER. That's one of the strangest things I've ever heard.

REBECCA. Well, it's true. The story is that my father was a violinist, and as a little girl I wanted to be a violinist too. Well, I wasn't wild about practicing, but I listened to music for hours on end. One day while I was in junior high, our stereo system began a strange rumbling sound in the middle of Mozart's flute and harp concerto.

INTERVIEWER. .... one of my favorite pieces of music.

REBECCA. Well, I still love it. I was frustrated about that rumbling, so I began to fiddle with the receiver. I wanted to see where it was coming from. You can't listen to Mozart with a rumble, after all. So I got out the wrenches and the screw drivers and began to check the transistors and the circuits one by one. Well, I didn't have a clue what I was doing and when my parents got home that night they were horrified to find the stereo in pieces all over the living room floor.

INTERVIEWER. Well, as a parent of a teenager myself, I can see why.

REBECCA. Yes, but you see, I was fascinated. The idea that a whole orchestra was in a little vacuum tube was magic to me. It was that night that my love affair with electricity really began. And I remember the wonderful confusion when it came time for me to go to college. Mother thought I should go to a music conservatory and become a violinist. She seemed to think that just because she always cried whenever I played "The Last Rose of Summer" that I was a brilliant musician in the making. Well, Dad was much more realistic about my talent and was convinced that I should study music history. So what did I do? I went to Georgia Tech.

INTERVIEWER. Georgia Tech. But that's not ...

REBECCA. Yeah, it's not. I went to Georgia tech to study electrical engineering.

INTERVIEWER. Well, why not. That made some sense.

REBECCA. Well, I thought so. My parents certainly didn't. Anyway what began to fascinate me at Georgia Tech was the idea that — how can I put this — well, the idea that electricity is not just energy in electrical form, but, actually, a type of information in electrical form.

INTERVIEWER. Well, I'll take your word for it.

REBECCA. Well, it thrilled me that I had a grasp of that. So I plunged into physics, math, everything there is that's connected with the study of electricity. But, by my junior year, I had been doing a lot of thinking and decided on a career in computer engineering. That made some sense, I thought. Now I had a background in electronics, and I thought I was interested not only in the software of computer work — that is, the writing of computer programs — but in the hardware, designing the computer system itself. By the middle of my senior year, I had pretty much decided to get a master's degree in systems engineering, a field that uses computers in the analysis and design of complex systems. Everyone agreed that I would make a good systems analyst.

INTERVIEWER. Hold it! You're going too fast for me. So far then, out of music, and out of the violin. in particular, into electrical engineering, is that right so far?

REBECCA. Yup, you've got it.

INTERVIEWER. Out of electrical engineering, then into computer engineering. And now you would go into systems engineering, is that it?

REBECCA. Right. But that's still just the beginning.

INTERVIEWER. Good heavens. Your parents must have been apoplectic.

REBECCA. Of course. They thought I should be committed to a loony bin.

INTERVIEWER. And that's only the beginning. Well, go on, go on, then what?

REBECCA. Well, I fooled everyone, including myself, and I got a master's degree in civil engineering.

INTERVIEWER. What?

REBECCA. Isn't that wild. Well, to tell you the truth, that strange sounding switch happened after I met John.

INTERVIEWER. John. There's a John in the picture!

REBECCA. Yes, there's a John in the picture. I was just finishing my bachelor's degree in computer engineering with my mind all made up about the future. I found myself at a cocktail party the day before graduation ....

INTERVIEWER. Oh, oh ....

REBECCA. .... and there I was talking to this perfect stranger ....

INTERVIEWER. I can see it coming ....

REBECCA. .... you know, your typical kind of cocktail party. Well, maybe he had too much to drink, but he made this outrageous statement that the only true form of engineering was civil engineering.

INTERVIEWER. Outrageous!

REBECCA. Well, that was an absurd thing to say. And I thought he was the most conceited and obstinate young man I'd ever met. Then, a month later I married him.

INTERVIEWER. Well, love is blind, they say. But he must have had some charm or other, some redeeming feature.

REBECCA. Charm and passion. He's a wonderful man. His true passion is for building things. He will talk forever, if you let him, about the intricacies and glories of putting up a building or laying down a road or raising a roof or lowering a tunnel. I had to take courses just to understand what John was talking about. I studied stress and contraction theories. I delved into the mysteries of reinforced concrete, and, finally, I did get my master's degree in civil engineering.

INTERVIEWER. Wow. Now at this point you were living in ....

REBECCA. .... here, in North Carolina.

INTERVIEWER. Oh, right here ...

REBECCA. John had taken a job with a large construction company in Durham. And I had come along with him as his wife and started my master's program at the University of North Carolina and finished it two years later. Now this is the embarrassing part. I had my master's degree, right?

INTERVIEWER. Right.

REBECCA. Well, when I sat down to think about my own career, I realized that I no longer knew what I wanted to do. So, of course, I became a teacher.

INTERVIEWER. A teacher. A teacher! At the university here?

REBECCA. Yes, at the University of North Carolina. Fortunately, it's not quite as strange as it may seem. You see, I had been a teaching assistant while I was getting my master's. And that paid my tuition. And I discovered that I really liked this teaching, and I was good at it. You know the old joke, "Those who can, do; those who can't teach." So there I was teaching part-time and also serving as assistant dean in the civil engineering department. It was great.

INTERVIEWER. Dean!

REBECCA. Yes, dean. Assistant dean. But isn't that impressive.

INTERVIEWER. Well, yes it is, as a matter of fact. I'd say awe-inspiring even.

REBECCA. Well, basically, I think I'm doing fine. I do a lot of student counseling and some curriculum work. I interview all the transfer students and help them make their adjustments to their new school. I also advise the international students. And I teach one or two labs each semester.

INTERVIEWER. Well, that's all well and good, but what I want to know about is the violin. What about the violin?

REBECCA. Interesting that you should ask. Are you free tomorrow night?

INTERVIEWER. Yeah, as a matter of fact.

REBECCA. I'm playing with a faculty group. We're all engineers of one kind or another. We're doing the Mozart Clarinet Quintet. Now it's an amateur group and we do it just for the fun of it, but for me working on the violin is a great way to let down, loosen up, and relax after a long hard day at the office. We're never going to play in Symphony Hall, you understand, but who cares.

INTERVIEWER. By gosh, Mozart. Back to Mozart. Beginning and ending with Mozart. I guess if it hadn't been for that Mozart rumble where would you be?

REBECCA. Yup! You can blame it all on Mozart.

Questions

The general comprehension questions, which are given in the student's book on page 77, should be discussed after the first listening to the interview.

Vocabulary in Context 2

Tape: Part Two — listening exercise

Listen to this recording and write down the word or phrase you hear. You will hear the word or phrase twice. Then, listen to two sentences in which that word or phrase is used. The second sentence is taken from the conversation you have just heard. Next, write down what you think that word or phrase means. Make an intelligent guess, using context clues.

1. **to be wild about**   **to be wild about**
   Example: Although he hadn't really wanted a child at that time, he was wild about the new baby and held her and played with her for hours at a time.
   From the tape: I wasn't wild about practicing, but I listened to music for hours on end.

2. **on end**   **on end**
   Example: When he first got his computer, he sat at the terminal for days on end, hardly taking time to sleep or eat.
   From the tape: I wasn't wild about practicing, but I listened to music for hours on end.

3. **to fiddle with**   **to fiddle with**
   Example: Please stop fiddling with that radio dial and leave it on one station. You're driving me crazy.
   From the tape: I was frustrated about that rumbling, so I began to fiddle with the receiver.

4. **in the making**   **in the making**
   Example: When their little boy was only six years old, they knew they had a great athlete in the making. He could run faster than boys who were five years older than he was.
   From the tape: Mother seemed to think that just because she always cried whenever I played "The Last Rose of Summer" on the violin, that I was a brilliant musician in the making.

5. **Hold it!**   **Hold it!**
   Example: Hold it! If you talk Spanish so quickly, I won't be able to understand a word.
   From the tape: Hold it, hold it! You're going too fast for me.

6. **a redeeming feature**   **a redeeming feature**
   Example: I agree with you that it is not a good university — the library is poor and most of the teachers are not well qualified. But it does have one redeeming feature: it's in Southern California, and the sun shines three hundred and fifty days a year.
   From the tape: Well, love is blind, they say. But he must have had some charm or other redeeming feature.

Definitions of vocabulary in context

1. **to be wild about**: ecstatic; overjoyed
2. **on end**: for a long time; without limit
3. **to fiddle with**: play with; handle nervously and repeatedly; move back and forth; tinker
4. **in the making**: soon to become; in process; forming; turning into
5. **hold it**: slow down; go more slowly; wait a minute; stop for a moment; stop
6. **a redeeming feature**: a positive aspect; a good quality

The Interview 1

Tape: Part One, again — the second listening

Rewind the tape and listen to the interview again. Then answer the following questions and do the reconstruction exercise.

Detailed Questions

These detailed comprehension questions may be asked after the second listening to the interview. They do not appear in the student's book?

1. Rebecca says, "I got into engineering because of my interest in music." Can you explain this.
2. Once Rebecca began her engineering studies, she rapidly moved from one field of engineering to another. What were the first three fields of engineering that Rebecca studied before she completed her bachelor's degree?
3. How did she become interested in civil engineering?
4. How did she qualify for her job as dean at the University of North Carolina?
5. Explain: "Those who can, do; those who can't, teach."
6. What five things does Rebecca do as dean?
7. Mozart begins and ends the interview. Explain.

Reconstruction

The exercise which is given in the student's book on page 78 should be done after the second listening to the interview.

The Dialogue ✺ 3

Tape: Part Three — A conversation between Rebecca and Budi

Lesson Eight, Rebecca Kraus, Asssistant Dean of Students, continues with the third part of the taped material, a dialogue between Rebecca and Budi Winotta, a foreign student in the university. We are in the dean's office. Listen to the dialogue and then answer the questions in your book.

BUDI (a student). You must be getting tired of seeing my face around here.

REBECCA. Not at all, Budi. Don't be silly. Now, what can I do for you this time?

BUDI. Well, same old thing, I guess. I'm thinking of switching majors again.

REBECCA. (*Laughing*) Regular as clockwork.

BUDI. Yeah, once a semester; you can count on it.

REBECCA. It's O.K. though; don't worry about it.

BUDI. But this is the third time. It's getting a little embarrassing.

REBECCA. Why? Why, good heavens, you're only twenty. I know people who changed their whole profession when they were over forty! Why worry about a little thing like changing your field in engineering?

BUDI. Well, I suppose it's just because I'm still not sure what I want.

REBECCA. Well, let's see now, you started out ...

BUDI. ..... in civil, but you know that was my parents. I wanted to do what my father did.

REBECCA. Happens all the time. Believe me, Budi, I was the same. Now then, let's see, you went into computers ...

BUDI. No, first it was mechanical engineering, but only for a while. *Then* I began to get into computer engineering. And I still like it O.K., but I'll tell you what really interests me; it's the hardware; it's the whole transistor world; it's circuits; it's ... when you come right down to it ... it's electricity.

REBECCA. Ah. I know the feeling. You sound like me in reverse.

BUDI. What do you mean?

REBECCA. Well, I started out in electrical engineering. Now I seem to be more and more interested in aspects of civil engineering. But electricity was my first love. (*Laughs*) Electricity and music.

BUDI. You're kidding! I can't believe it!

REBECCA. Can't believe what?

BUDI. Well, music. I mean ... see ... the truth is, my secret interest is in electronic music. That's why I wanted to do more in electrical engineering.

REBECCA. Well, I'll be!

BUDI. See? It's crazy! Half of me wants to go to a music school!

REBECCA. I don't think that's crazy at all.

BUDI. You don't? But it's completely illogical!

REBECCA. Ah, don't let that stop you. We all have an inner logic. I love those wonderful lines by poet Conrad Aiken. He said, "Order in all things, logic in the dark, arrangement in the atom and the spark, time in the heart, and sequence in the brain." Now, I don't mean to quote poetry at you, but he was right, you know.

BUDI. Then you really think I should go to a music school?

REBECCA. Well, I wouldn't rush it. Wait a year. Learn some more about electricity. See how you feel. Then, if you want to go to a music school, well, why not? You only live once!

Questions

The discussion questions given in the student's book on page 79 should be used after listening to the dialogue.

The Interactive Listening 4

Tape: Part Four — A listening comprehension test

This is a multiple choice test. It is similar in construction to the listening section of the Michigan Test or the TOEFL test except that all of the information is about engineers and engineering. The information has been taken from the Occupational Outlook Handbook 1988-1989 Edition, published by U.S. Department of Labor and Bureau of Labor Statistics. Listen carefully to the statement on the tape. Choose the one statement in your book — a, b, or c — that is closest in meaning to the statement you have heard. Mark your answers on the answer sheet in your student's book on page 81.

1. Employment of metalurgical, ceramics, and materials engineers is expected to grow faster than the average for all occupations through the year 2000.
2. Employment of mining engineers is expected to remain level through the year 2000 due to expected low growth in demand for coal, metals, and other minerals.
3. Civil engineers held 199,000 jobs in 1986. Almost forty percent of the jobs were in federal, state, and local government agencies.
4. Since only a small proportion of the oil and gas in a reservoir will flow out under natural forces, petroleum engineers develop and use various enhanced recovery methods, such as flooding the oilfield with water to force more of the oil out of the reservoir. The best methods in use today recover only about half the oil in a reservoir. Petroleum engineers work to find ways to increase this proportion.
5. Employment of nuclear engineers is expected to change little through the year 2000. Almost all job openings will result from the need to replace nuclear engineers who retire or leave the occupation. Despite the expected absence of growth, there are expected to be good opportunities for nuclear engineers because the number of new graduates with degrees in nuclear engineering is small and has been declining recently.
6. A bachelor's degree in engineering from an accredited engineering program is generally acceptable for beginning engineering jobs.
7. Starting salaries for engineers with bachelor's degrees are significantly higher than starting salaries of college graduates in other fields.
8. Since many electrical engineering jobs are defense related, cutbacks in defense spending could result in layoffs.
9. Engineers in high-technology areas such as advanced electronics or aerospace may find that their knowledge becomes obsolete rapidly.
10. Engineers should be able to work as a team and should have creativity, open minds, and a capacity for detail. All engineers should be able to express themselves well — both orally and in writing.

Answers to the interactive listening exercise

1. b   2. c   3. b   4. a   5. c   6. c   7. b   8. b   9. c   10. b

The Projects

A choice of communicative activities

The projects are designed to be done concurrently with the listening work. The explanations for the projects start on page 82 of the student's book.

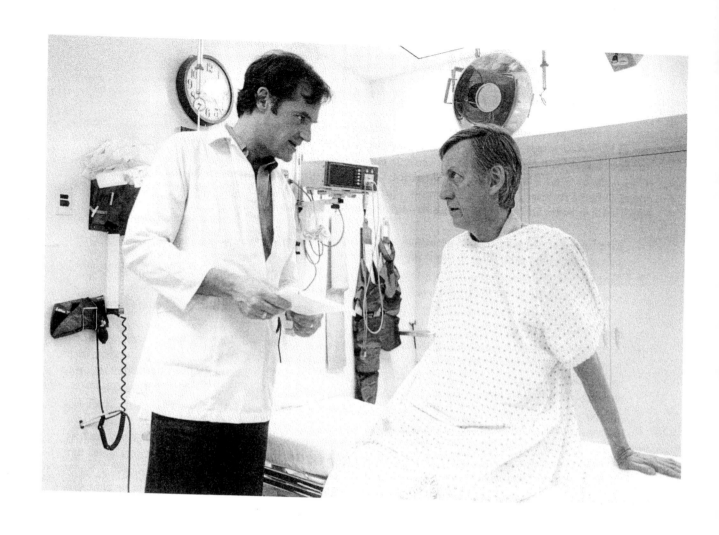

Lesson Nine

Tom Hyatt
Medical Intern

This chapter is about a doctor. Most of the related vocabulary is very important to all students because it deals with doctors, hospitals, accidents and disease. You can expand on it. For example, the medical form that the student fills out during the interactive listening could be fully discussed. Issues such as hospital insurance, the *closest hospitals, parts of the body, etc. can be included here. Our own experience has been that students often learn names of parts of the body in a beginning class, and it is not taught again. Students who have to describe symptoms to a doctor rarely have the vocabulary for internal organs.*

Introductory Reading ✍

This reading, which is given in the student's book on page 87, should be discussed as a prelistening exercise.

Work Related Vocabulary — with definitions

1. a **surgeon**: a physician specializing in surgery

2. **surgery**: treatment of injury or disease by instrumental operation

3. a **general practitioner**: a doctor in general practice who provides primary care only but treats a wide variety of ailments. In many small towns, the only doctor is a general practitioner (G.P.) who does everything from delivering babies to setting broken bones. G.P.s provide care for every member of the family regardless of age so they are often called family doctors.

4. an **emergency ward**: a hospital unit that provides care for accident victims and persons who have suddenly become ill

5. to **commit suicide**: to intentionally kill oneself

6. **unconscious**: temporarily lacking full awareness as in a coma or deep sleep

7. a **heart attack**: the condition or an instance of heart failure; any seizure or abnormal heart functioning

8. an **ambulance**: an automobile or other vehicle especially equipped to transport the sick and wounded

9. an **electrocardiograph**: a machine which records the electrical impulses of the heart

10. a **massive coronary**: a very serious heart attack

11. **intensive care**: care given in a special hospital unit to patients who are very ill and require constant observation by doctors and nurses

12. **in shock**: a state of massive physiological reaction to bodily trauma — generally temporary — usually characterized by marked loss of blood pressure and depression of vital processes

13. **x-ray**: (Roentgen) rays, which cannot be seen, penetrate the human body and leave a record upon a photographic plate which makes it possible for doctors to diagnose the medical problems of patients

14. **pelvic**: (of, in or near the pelvis) The pelvis is an area in the lower part of the body resting on the legs and supporting the spinal column. It is made up of bones on the side, the pubis in front, and the sacrum and coccyx behind.

15. a **dislocated shoulder**: a bone has been displaced from the socket in the shoulder

16. **sprains**: a painful pulling of the ligaments of a joint such as the ankle or wrist or knee

17. **cuts**: an opening or incision in the skin which often bleeds, caused by something sharp.

18. **bruises**: a surface wound that doesn't cut the skin; a discoloration of the skin after a dull or hard blow to it; this often is a blue mark (called "black and blue") on the skin which gradually changes color as it heals

19. **suture work**: a sewing together of deep cuts after injury or operation with thread or gut or wire

20. **setting bones**: putting bones together which have broken as a result of an injury and leaving them bound for periods of time so they will heal in a straightened position

21. **stitches**: the loops made by a thread when sewing; in this context the loops made by thread, wire, or gut in order to join two areas of the body together after an injury or operation

22. a **pediatrician**: a doctor specializing in the care of infants and children and the treatment of their diseases

23. an **obstetrician**: a doctor specializing in the care of women during pregnancy, childbirth, and any recuperative period following delivery of the baby

24. a **gynecologist**: a doctor specializing in the diseases of the reproductive organs and the endocrinology of women

The Interview ✳ 1

Tape: Part One — The first listening

Lesson Nine of People at Work begins with a conversation with medical intern, Tom Hyatt. Before listening, review the work related vocabulary in your book. You will listen to the interview at least twice. After the first listening, answer the questions in your book and then do the vocabulary in context exercise, using both your book and this tape. When you have finished the vocabulary in context, rewind and listen to the conversation with Tom again.

Tom leads a very busy life as a medical intern. At the moment, he is in the bathtub. He has just finished rereading a letter which he got earlier today from his uncle Ed, and now, even though he's taking a bath, he picks up the phone and dials long distance.

INTERVIEWER. Hello?

TOM. Uncle Ed?

INTERVIEWER. Tom! This is a surprise!

TOM. Am I interrupting anything? Is this a good time to talk?

INTERVIEWER. Well, sure, any time. This is great. What's up.

TOM. Well, I just got your letter, and I read it today over lunch. I wanted to get right back to you, but, you know, with my impossible schedule I was afraid I'd let it slip. So here I am, sitting in the bathtub, using the phone instead.

INTERVIEWER. What? In the bathtub? You mean, taking a bath?

TOM. Yup. Right now. You've got to picture this. Here I am sitting in hot water up to here, with this board across the tub, sort of like a table. And I've got the cordless phone on it and my supper, right here balanced on the board.

INTERVIEWER. Really?

TOM. Yup. Fried chicken and fries and coleslaw, which I just picked up at Kentucky Fried Chicken. You see, this way I get to do three things at once, maybe even four or five things. It's become a way of life.

INTERVIEWER. Well, I hope you don't ever try to do all that driving around in a car.

TOM. Oh, if I could find a car with a bathtub in it that would be perfect. Now, about your letter. I didn't realize that my dear cousin, Steve, has definitely decided to go to medical school.

INTERVIEWER. Well, that's what it looks like. We're all surprised.

TOM. Terrific! Good for him. But what's all this that I should convince him to become a surgeon. I don't get it. Why do you want me to do that?

INTERVIEWER. Why? Simple. Because there's more money in it, and because it's a lot more interesting.

TOM. More money? Not necessarily. And more interesting? More interesting than what?

INTERVIEWER. Well, Tom, more interesting than general practice. You know what I mean!

TOM. No, I don't. More interesting than general practice? Whatever makes you say that? Do you think if Steve became a general practitioner he'd get bored?

INTERVIEWER. Well ... that's not exactly what I was ....

TOM. Nothing could be further from the truth. Really, nothing. Hey, let me tell you about last night in the emergency ward. That's where I've been now for three weeks.

INTERVIEWER. Tom, I'm not saying that ....

TOM. Just listen ... first of all, I came on duty at 11:30 at night. Just after midnight, this police rescue squad comes in with a married couple, both of them in pretty bad shape. The woman had tried to commit suicide, you know, swallowing a bottle of aspirin — while her husband was watching TV. He finds her lying there unconscious on their bedroom floor. He was pretty shook up, of course, and while he was on the phone calling the police emergency number, he has a heart attack — right there, on the phone. Luckily it was mild, and he had already reached the police about his wife ... so a police ambulance was there at the house in no time ... .

86

INTERVIEWER. Tom, you know, I never said it would be boring ... all I said was that ....

TOM. But wait. There's more. Just as we were connecting the husband to an electrocardiograph machine, the head nurse tells us that another heart attack victim is being admitted at the very moment. And this is the real thing: a massive coronary. The nurse takes over at the electrocardiograph, and we run like hell to help the new patient. O.K. So now we have three patients under intensive care.

INTERVIEWER. Look Tom, when I said it wasn't as interesting as surgery ....

TOM. Let me finish. Well, at 2:30 a.m. all hell breaks loose. The police bring in eight young men who've been in a bad accident: motor cycle — car collision. It was unbelievable. They are in their black leather jackets, man, and drunk, wiped out. And in shock, of course. We x-ray one who has a serious pelvic injury and send him to emergency surgery. The other injuries are not so severe, but there are a lot of them: broken fingers, dislocated shoulders, sprains, cuts, bruises. And a lot of blood. I mean a lot of blood. I worked for three hours straight out, without stopping — mainly suture work and setting bones. I took enough stitches to make an overcoat. Uncle Ed, that's a joke. Get it.

INTERVIEWER. That's a terrible joke, Tom.

TOM. Anyway, by the time I got off duty at 5:30, I was shaking with exhaustion.

INTERVIEWER. All right, all right. I get it. Nevertheless, what you are describing isn't just everyone's cup of tea, you know.

TOM. Of course not. I guess what I'm really saying is that we can't predict right now what Steve is going to find the most appropriate or interesting branch of medicine. He'll have plenty of chance to figure all that out for himself once the course work begins and ....

INTERVIEWER. .... and so you're saying in your nice, polite way that maybe I should be letting Steve find his own way ... through all this.

TOM. Well, you know. He already has his own dreams, and he's finding his way. He's young. I remember when I was Steve's age, just beginning med school, I was sure I wanted to be a surgeon, dead sure. Then a pediatrician. Then an obstetrician or maybe a gynecologist. The truth is I didn't really know what I wanted to be. It takes time — a long time sometimes — and experience to find out. Everything you learn is interesting and confuses the situation. Right now it seems likely that I'll end up in general practice. Why? I don't know. I guess I like the idea of just being able to deal with anything that goes wrong with another human being — medically, that is.

INTERVIEWER. Well, Tom, this is all something to think about. But I shouldn't hold you up any longer. Say, how's that bath water. It must be getting pretty cold in there!

TOM. Cold? Oh my gosh, cold. Brrr. I feel like a penguin. And not only that. I think I've been eating the soap along with the fries.

INTERVIEWER. Well, before you freeze to death or start blowing bubbles, it's time to get off. Oh, and Aunt Bess sends her love. Steve will want to get together with you and talk this all out, I'm sure. And maybe when he hears the truth about all this, you'll talk him out of medicine altogether. What a wild profession.

TOM. I think I did eat the soap. Bye!

INTERVIEWER. Gech mish olsun! That's Turkish for "Let it pass quickly."

Questions

The general comprehension questions which are given in the student's book on page 89 should be discussed after the first listening to the interview.

Vocabulary in Context ✱ 2

Tape: Part Two — listening exercise

Listen to this recording and write down the word or phrase you hear. You will hear the word or phrase twice. Then, listen to two sentences in which that word or phrase is used. The second sentence is taken from the conversation you've just heard. Next, write down what you think that word means. Make an intelligent guess, using context clues.

1. **what's up?**   **what's up?**
   Example: My brother almost always starts a conversation by saying, "Hey, what's up?"
   From the tape: This is great. What's up?

2. **let [something] slip**   **let [something] slip**
   Example: I'm in real trouble with my boss. He wanted the work by two o'clock today, but I forgot about it and let it slip, so it wasn't ready.
   From the tape: With my impossible schedule, I was afraid I'd let it slip.

3. **to pick up**   **to pick up**
   Example: Do you like this new jacket I'm wearing? I picked it up at a sale last week.
   From the tape: Chicken and fries and coleslaw which I just picked up at Kentucky Fried Chicken.

4. **I don't get it.**   **I don't get it.**
   Example: Everyone else is laughing at John's joke. Maybe it's funny, but I don't get it.
   From the tape: I don't get it. Why do you want me to do that?

5. **shook up**   **shook up**
   Example: When the car crashed into the tree, luckily they were not hurt. But they were very shook up.
   From the tape: He finds her lying there unconscious on their bedroom floor. He was pretty shook up, of course.

6. **to run like hell**   **to run like hell**
   Example: When he saw the angry dog coming towards him, he ran like hell.
   From the tape: The nurse took over at the electrocardiograph, and we ran like hell to help the new patient.

Additional vocabulary

7. **all hell breaks loose**   **all hell breaks loose**
   Example: All hell broke loose: some students were running around, others were throwing their books, some were even fighting with each other.
   From the tape: At 2:30 a.m. all hell breaks loose.

8. **to get off duty**   **to get off duty**
   Example: This week I start work every day at 2 p.m. and I get off duty 8 hours later at 10.
   From the tape: By the time I got off duty at 5:30 I was shaking with exhaustion.

9. **cup of tea**   **cup of tea**
   Example: I'm sorry, but swimming in very cold ocean water is just not my cup of tea.
   From the tape: What you are describing isn't just everyone's cup of tea.

10. **dead sure**   **dead sure**
    Example: I am dead sure that my car won't start. I've been trying to start it unsuccessfully for two hours.
    From the tape: I was sure I wanted to be a surgeon. Dead sure.

11. **to end up   to end up**
    Example: If John doesn't take care of his health, he's going to end up in the hospital.
    From the tape: Now it seems likely that I'll end up an internist.

12. **to hold up   to hold up**
    Example: I'm very late. I feel terrible. I'm afraid I've held you up. I know you wanted to be downtown by five o'clock.
    From the tape: I shouldn't hold you up any longer.

13. **to get off   to get off**
    Example: I'm sorry. I have to get off the phone. There's a whole line of people waiting to use it.
    From the tape: Well, before you freeze to death or start blowing bubbles, it's time to get off.

14. **to talk out   to talk out**
    Example: We haven't had enough time to discuss this matter. Let's get together again and talk it out.
    From the tape: Steve will want to get together with you and talk this out.

Definitions of vocabulary in context

1. What's happening? What's new? It's often used as a greeting at the beginning of a conversation: "Hi, What's up?"
2. to forget about doing something that one intended to do; to omit; to neglect
3. to buy quickly and casually and often without prior intention
4. I don't understand this.
5. emotionally upset
6. to run very fast
7. Many things happen at once which cause disturbance, uproar, trouble, chaos, riotous conditions.
8. to finish work or end one's post in such places as a hospital or the military
9. something one likes; something related to one's knowledge
10. absolutely certain; one hundred percent certain
11. to reach one's final goal or state
12. to delay someone or something
13. to say goodbye, hang up, and end one's telephone conversation
14. to discuss thoroughly all aspects of a topic

The Interview 1

Tape: Part One, again — The second listening

Rewind the tape and listen to the interview again. Then answer the following questions and do the reconstruction exercise.

Detailed Questions

These detailed comprehension questions may be asked after the second listening to the interview. They do not appear in the student's book.

1. From all the clues that you find in the conversation between Tom and Uncle Ed, reconstruct the letter that Ed had written Tom before this conversation takes place.
2. From what you understand, what was the major point of Uncle Ed's letter to Steve.
3. During this conversation, how many things is Tom doing at once?
4. In his conversation with Uncle Ed, what is Tom's major point about Steve's future?
5. Discuss Tom's eating habits.
6. "What a wild profession!" Why does he say this?
7. List the patients whom Tom saw in the emergency room and briefly describe why each had come there.
8. What is the controversy between Tom and Uncle Ed?
9. What do you learn about Steve in this conversation?
10. What do you learn about Uncle Ed (the interviewer) in this conversation?

Reconstruction

The exercise which is given in the student's book on page 90 should be done after the second listening to the interview.

The Dialogue 1

Tapes: Part Three — A conversation between Tom and Steve

Listen to the conversation and then answer the questions in your book.

TOM. Hello.

STEVE. Tom, this is Steve.

TOM. Steve, wow. It's great to hear from you. How're you doing, cousin.

STEVE. Great, and I promise I'll make this quick, cuz I know you're probably in the middle of doing three things at once, and you're probably heading out to the hospital, right?

TOM. Hey, I've got all the time in the world. Ten minutes. Besides, I'm waiting for my frozen dinner to cook, so tell me, what's up?

STEVE. Well, Dad tells me you two had a long talk on the subject of my future.

TOM. Right, and what's this about your thinking about becoming a doctor? I had no idea. I didn't know you had such good sense.

STEVE. Hey, it runs in the family. But Tom, that's the thing. That's the problem. I don't know where dad got this "surgeon" idea. Because the truth is I haven't really decided what I want to do... what I want to be ... ya know? I mean, I'm not really sure right now that I even want to be a doctor.

TOM. Aha.

STEVE. I mean, I'm interested and all, but I'm interested in a lot of other things too.

TOM. ... like photography, for instance.

STEVE. Yeah, exactly. You know all about that?

TOM. Sure I do. I don't think I can remember ever seeing you without a camera slung around your neck.

STEVE. It's getting worse. This year I'm taking practically all the pictures for the school yearbook. I've built my own darkroom, and I'm up to my armpits in negatives.

TOM. Terrific! And that just goes to prove what I was telling your dad. It's early yet to decide what you're going to do with your life. After all, you're only ... what ... seventeen ... years old ....

STEVE. Eighteen.

TOM. O.K., eighteen. You don't need to commit yourself yet. I guess you already know that. But that's what I've been telling your dad. Look, you'll start at the university, you can take some pre-med courses like chemistry, biology, and other courses too: art, geology, history ... and you'll find your way, testing out what you really like and what you're really good at.

STEVE. Well, that makes sense.

TOM. .... and now as we're talking, I'm thinking. You know, I've got a classmate here in med school whose specialization is in medical photography.

STEVE. Medical photography?

TOM. Yeah, and there are different kinds of medical photography. There's one called tomography. They're using it as a diagnostic tool for cancer. It's right there at the cutting edge in cancer research. Medical photography.

STEVE. Wow, that's something to think about. Tom, old buddy, you're a genius.

TOM. You're just saying that because it's true. O.K., so the bottom line in what I'm trying to say is, come on, it's early yet. Give yourself some time ... stay open to the possibilities. Don't let your dad ... you know what I mean.

STEVE. Sure, I got you. But you know dad, he seems to think that ....

TOM. Oh my god, my frozen dinner is suddenly ... is ... is ....

STEVE. ... burning ...?

TOM. Burning!

STEVE. Try to rescue it. Now, we've got to get together ....

TOM. (cough cough cough) .... oh the smoke in here. Have you ever tasted rescued chicken? Give my love to the family! Bye.

STEVE. Bye.

Questions

The discussion questions given in the student's book on page 91 should be used after listening to the dialogue.

The Interactive Listening 4

Tape: Part Four — Filling out a medical history form.

In this exercise, you will listen to an interview between Dr. Rose and Mrs. Gold, who is seeing the doctor for the first time. Imagine that you are the doctor and fill out information on Mrs. Gold on the medical history form given in your student's book on page 92.

DR. ROSE. Mrs. Gold, how do you do. I'm Dr. Rose.

MRS. GOLD. How do you do. I've been looking for a new doctor, and Harry and Sarah Webster highly recommend you.

DR. ROSE. Oh, the Websters. They're old friends and patients of mine. Say hello to them for me when you see them. In the meantime, what brings you here today?

MRS. GOLD. Well, I haven't been feeling terrific lately. It's hard to put my finger on it. I've had some bad headaches which I've never had before, and my stomach's been upset. Also I feel tired all the time.

DR. ROSE. Well, we'll give you a complete examination in a few minutes. But now, would you fill me in on some background and family history. First of all, your full name.

MRS. GOLD. Elizabeth Gold.

DR. ROSE. And how old are you, Mrs. Gold?

MRS. GOLD. Forty-four next month. Is that possible? Yes, forty-four.

DR. ROSE. Married?

MRS. GOLD. Yes, for twenty years.

DR. ROSE. Children?

MRS. GOLD. Two girls, both in high school, Mary, age sixteen, and Joan, age forteen.

DR. ROSE. Are your parents alive?

MRS. GOLD. My mother is. She's 67. My father died five years ago.

DR. ROSE. And the cause of his death . . . .

MRS. GOLD. He had lung cancer. He was a heavy smoker to the end.

DR. ROSE. Do you smoke, Mrs. Gold?

MRS. GOLD. I used to, but I stopped several years ago.

DR. ROSE. Is your mother in good health?

MRS. GOLD. Quite good for a woman of her age, except for some arthritis.

DR. ROSE. Has anyone in your family had diabetes?

MRS. GOLD. Well, I have an aunt who has it.

DR. ROSE. What about cancer?

MRS. GOLD. No one except for my father — I told you about that.

DR. ROSE. Right. And what about heart trouble.

MRS. GOLD. Hmm. I think my great-grandfather had some heart problems, but I'm not sure.

DR. ROSE. Let me ask you . . . are you taking any medication?

MRS. GOLD. No, not really. I've been taking a lot of aspirin for the headaches and some over-the-counter medication for my upset stomach.

DR. ROSE. Have you had any operations or serious illnesses?

MRS. GOLD. I had my gall bladder out five years ago, but except for that and for having babies, that's it.

DR. ROSE. Have you had frequent colds or sore throats?

MRS. GOLD. Not especially. Just the one or two that everyone gets in the winter around here.

DR. ROSE. What about allergies?

MRS. GOLD. No, none that I can think of, except for seafood. I break out in a rash even if I go near it.

DR. ROSE. And what about allergies to medication?

MRS. GOLD. No, nothing that I know of.

DR. ROSE. Have you been worried about anything lately, Mrs. Gold.

MRS. GOLD. Hm . . . well, no more than usual, I suppose. One of my daughters is giving me some problems, nothing really serious. And, of course, everyone has financial worries, but I don't think I'm overly worried or depressed about anything.

DR. ROSE. Okay, Mrs. Gold. Why don't you step on the scale and we'll see how much you weigh.

MRS. GOLD. Now that is something to be depressed about.

Medical History

NAME *Elizabeth Gold*   AGE *44*

ADDRESS _____   HEIGHT _____

2 children   WEIGHT _____

Please check (✓) any of these
problems that you have had:

Frequent colds *usual winter*
Frequent sore throats *usual winter*
Frequent headaches *✓*
Allergies *seafood*
Stomach problems *✓*
Kidney problems _____
High blood pressure _____
Anemia _____
Mental depression _____
Serious injuries _____
Heart condition _____

Please check (✓) any of these
diseases that you have had:

Chickenpox _____
Measles _____
Rubella _____
Mumps _____
Scarlet Fever _____
Polio _____
Whooping Cough _____
Tuberculosis _____
Diabetes _____
Hepatitis _____
Ulcers _____
Epilepsy _____

Are you taking any medications? _____
Which ones? *Aspirin - Over the counter medication for stomach*
Are you allergic to any medications? _____
Which ones? _____
Have you had any operations? *Gall Bladder*
Please describe them briefly and give the dates: _____

_____

Have you ever been hospitalized for any other reason? *2 children*
Please describe briefly and give the dates: _____
Does anyone have or has anyone in your family had:

WHO   RELATION

Diabetes   *Aunt*
Cancer   *Father, Lung Cancer - smoker*
Heart condition   *Great Grandfather ??*

Other information: *Stopped smoking several years ago*
Tired   Gall Bladder

The Projects

A choice of communicative activities

The projects are designed to be done concurrently with the listening work. The explanations for the projects start on page 93 of the student's book.

Lesson Ten

Connie Snow

Building Contractor

Note to the teacher or tutor:

In this chapter, Connie Snow, a builder, has also reached her new job through a roundabout route. She is interested in it because of the many varied things it gives her the opportunity to do, as well as the feeling that she is doing something useful.

The vocabulary in the first section should be useful to all students whether they are in the building trades or not. A teacher could expand this vocabulary section by including names of other tools that most people use in their homes.

The projects are concerned with housing, one of the basic needs. Students may be very interested in

other housing issues that arise during this chapter.

In the interactive listening exercise, students draw a picture following a description given on the tape. Students may want to write their own descriptions telling their fellow students what to draw. They can either dictate these or tape them.

It is possible that students will be concerned with Connie's pronunciation of "houses." This gives you a chance to point out that some regional dialects of English may vary from what they have been taught is "correct."

Introductory Reading ❧

This reading, which is given in the student's book on page 97, should be discussed as a prelistening exercise.

Work Related Vocabulary — with definitions

1. a **hammer**: a hand tool with a solid round top, usually metal, used to drive in nails and to pound down on things
    a **saw**: a hand or electric-powered tool with a thin, flat blade and a continuous series of "teeth" designed for cutting wood and other materials.
2. a **contractor**: builder, supplier, one who contracts to build; one who performs work or provides supplies for an agreed price.
3. **speculation**: entering into a financially risky business arrangement for a chance at an unusually large profit
4. **preplanning**: making plans for building designs and architecture before any large financial investment or before construction takes place
5. **a building site**: any land, lot, or property used to build any type of structure — single-family house, apartment building, or high-rise office building
6. **mortgage money**: money loaned by a bank or lending institution to a property owner so that the owner can take possession of the property immediately, then repay the bank's loan on the "mortgaged" property with interest over a specified period of time
7. **a subcontractor**: an individual or business firm that contracts and is paid to perform a specified part of the work or to provide specified materials, for the main or "prime" contractor
8. **a low interest rate**: a percentage rate of interest that is considered lower, at a particular date, than the current interest rate being charged by most banks and lending institutions
9. **a credit rating**: a rating system established by financial service organizations, lending institutions, businesses, and stores to determine the financial reliability and ability to pay of an individual or business that wants to borrow money "on credit" to be repaid with interest over a period of time
10. **monthly payments**: the amount of money, including principle and interest, that must be paid each month by an individual or business to a bank or lending institution for money loaned
11. **a foundation**: the whole substructure, usually made of reinforced concrete and sometimes iron, underneath a building or structure and upon which that structure is built and supported
12. **framing**: the constructional system that gives shape and strength to a building; the arrangement of supporting girders, beams, columns, joists, and trusses that form the main support of a building

Additional vocabulary

1. **macho**: a male sexist attitude; an excessive show of masculinity or manly virility, often in conversational style or personal appearance, suggesting male superiority or dominance over women
2. to **screen**: to select after examining, inspecting, investigating or considering several choices
3. **eligible**: qualified; capable; suitable; satisfactory; worthy of being chosen
4. **disgruntled**: not satisfied; upset; in a bad mood

95

The Interview ✳ 1

Tape: Part One — The first listening

Lesson Ten of People at Work begins with an interview with building contractor, Connie Snow. Before listening, review the work related vocabulary in your book on page 98. You will listen to the interview at least twice. After the first listening, answer the questions in your book and then do the vocabulary in context exercise, using both your book and this tape. When you have finished the vocabulary in context, rewind and listen to the interview with Connie again. The interview takes place out at a building site. Bonnie and Ed are sitting on a couple of saw horses. Please forgive all the noise in the background. Now, Connie Snow, building contractor.

INTERVIEWER. Well frankly, I was expecting someone a little older, a little bit macho maybe.

CONNIE. Macho? Oh, I can be macho if I have to.

INTERVIEWER. Well, I'll take your word for it. Now, I am right, aren't I, that you are the contractor for this building project?

CONNIE. Right. I'm the contractor and also the supervisor. And you understand, don't you, that this is a "self-help housing program?"

INTERVIEWER. Well, that's what you said, but I'm not quite sure what you mean by "self-help housing program."

CONNIE. What it boils down to is that I help families build their own houses. As you can see, there are eight houses here, so I'm working with these eight families. And right now we're into the third month of the project.

INTERVIEWER. I like it. I like it. You know, that's something I always thought I'd like to do someday ... to build my own house. But I just can't imagine actually doing it. And you're working on all the eight houses, all at the same time? Is that right?

CONNIE. Right. Right. Do you know anything about building?

INTERVIEWER. Well, I know a hammer and a saw when I see them, and that's about it.

CONNIE. Well, believe it or not, it's the same story with many of these families I'm working with. Most of these people don't have any experience with building.

INTERVIEWER. I just don't see how you can do all this with inexperienced people. There must be a lot of headaches for you.

CONNIE. Oh sure, like anything else, I guess. But I think I've learned to live with the headaches. The project is really pretty exciting.

INTERVIEWER. Well, I can see why. Here we have the Great American Dream. We all want to own our own houses. And that's what you're helping these people do. And that's exciting.

CONNIE. It is. You know these days, what with inflation, the high cost of materials and labor, and speculation in the housing market, a lot of people don't even think about home ownership.

INTERVIEWER. I realize I should tell my son and his new wife about this. They want to own their own home. They certainly don't want to go on renting forever. And they certainly can't afford one unless they build it themselves.

CONNIE. Let's talk about that later.

INTERVIEWER. Good. Now I want to know more about your involvement with this project. What's your role in all this?

CONNIE. I'm up to my ears from the very beginning 'til the very end. Let me explain. At the beginning, I'm responsible for all the preplanning. That means I buy all the building sites; I make arrangements with the Farmer's Home Administration ....

INTERVIEWER. Hold it. The Farmer's Home Administration? What's that?

CONNIE. Yes, yes, it acts like the bank; it lends mortgage money to the families. Then I line up the subcontractors.

INTERVIEWER. Oop op op ... you're going too fast for me ... so, in order to get into this project, let's see if I understand this, the families have to borrow money, is that it? And from Farmer's Home Administration.

CONNIE. Right.

INTERVIEWER. And apparently you don't have to be a farmer to borrow that money.

CONNIE. That's right. Anyone with a low income, living in a rural area is eligible. Now, after that I screen the families and decide which ones we'll let into the project.

INTERVIEWER. Who can get in?

CONNIE. There are lots of things we consider. First of all, the total income of the family can't be more than $18,000 a year. These days that's considered to be low income. Next, I need to be quite sure that the family has a real commitment to the project; I mean, are they really going to be willing and able to put in thirty hours of work a week on the houses?

INTERVIEWER. Thirty hours a week! Are you serious!? Gosh, that seems like a lot of time! Don't most of these people have full-time jobs away from here?

CONNIE. They sure do.

INTERVIEWER. Well, then how do they do it? Can other people, maybe friends, family ... can they ...

CONNIE. ... help them? Oh sure, that's the thing. It can be fathers, mothers, children, cousins, brothers, sisters, friends — whatever — and everyone's time counts toward those thirty hours a week.

INTERVIEWER. Oh well, that's great. But even so, there must be a lot of emotional strain on these couples.

CONNIE. There sure is. I have to be very careful to choose couples where it's clear that the marriages are strong. I mean, these are difficult days: the family adding construction work on top of full-time jobs and, in many cases, raising one ... two ... maybe three kids.

INTERVIEWER. Well frankly, I just don't see how they do it. So, anyway, after you've screened the families, then what happens?

CONNIE. Then the approved families go off to Farmer's Home Administration. As I said, that's where they have to get approval to borrow the money.

INTERVIEWER. ..... just ... oh, I just want to ask about the money. How much ... about how much money do they borrow?

CONNIE. It takes about $60,000 to build one of these houses.

INTERVIEWER. And what about the interest they pay on that money. Do they pay a very low interest rate?

CONNIE. The interest can be as low as 1%, depending on family income.

INTERVIEWER. Hm. 1%! That's a good deal. What a deal. Wow! Now can just anyone borrow that money?

CONNIE. No. Not really. When they go to Farmer's Home, the family has to be able to prove first that they're low income, and also that they have a good credit rating, you know, that when they've borrowed money in the past — buying a car, washing machine, whatever — that they were regular and faithful about making their monthly payment. Then, once they have that approval, they come back to me to choose the land they want ... from the various lots I purchase for the project.

INTERVIEWER. Uh huh, I see. You said before that you've been working about three months out here at this site. I see you've done a lot. Can you tell me a little bit about how you organize all this?

CONNIE. Well, I have it organized so that all the familes work together as a group on Tuesday and Thursday evenings for five hours each night; then on Saturdays and Sundays, we work for another ten hours each day. With this particular project, in the first week we did the foundations for the eight houses. Then we went on to the house of the first family and did the framing, and so on until ...

INTERVIEWER. ..... you had done all the framing for all the houses.

CONNIE. That's it. Then on to the roofing for each house, and it goes on like that 'til we finish all the houses.

INTERVIEWER. How long do you figure the whole project is going to take, from beginning to end? A year .... year and a half...?

CONNIE. About a year ... to complete all eight houses. And by that time, believe me, I'm sure we'll have a lot of disgruntled and exhausted people.

INTERVIEWER. But I can imagine how satisfying it is for a family to be able to say, "By gosh, we built this gorgeous house with our own hands."

CONNIE. That is, with a little help from our friends and from Farmer's Home Administration.

INTERVIEWER. And from Connie ....

CONNIE. Well, yeah, and Connie. I hope they'll add that.

Questions

The general comprehension qustions which are given in the student's book on page 99 should be discussed after the first listening to the interview.

Vocabulary in Context ✳ 2

Tape: Part Two — Listening exercise

Listen to this recording and write down the word or phrase you hear. You will hear the word or phrase twice. Then, listen to two sentences in which that word or phrase is used. The second sentence is taken from the conversation you have just heard. Next, write down what you think that word or phrase means. Make an intelligent guess, using context clues.

1. **to take one's word for**   **to take one's word for**
   Example: I really can't prove it. You'll just have to take my word for it.
   From the tape: I'll take your word for it.

2. **to boil down to**   **to boil down to**
   Example: You say you don't like the way I comb my hair and you don't like my clothes and you don't like the way I talk. What it boils down to is that you just don't like me.
   From the tape: What it boils down to is that I help families build their own houses.

3. **up to one's ears**   **up to one's ears**
   Example: I'm really sorry I can't go with you to the party. But I'm up to my ears in work, and you know I just wouldn't enjoy it.
   From the tape: I'm up to my ears from the beginning through to the very end.

4. **on top of**   **on top of**
   Example: I'll never be ready for my guests. On top of all the cleaning, I haven't even started to fix dinner.
   From the tape: These are difficult days … the family adding construction work on top of full-time jobs.

5. **to line up**   **to line up**
   Example: In my job I can't pay people to do all of the necessary research, so I have to line up a lot of volunteers.
   From the tape: Then I line up the subcontractors.

6. **to count on**   **to count on**
   Example: We can always count on Maria. When she says she'll be here at eight o'clock, she's here at eight o'clock, or even before.
   From the tape: We are counting on at least two people in the family to be working at the same time.

Definitions of vocabulary in context

1. to accept a statement as truthful, to believe fully, to be convinced of
2. to simplify, to summarize, to decrease a large amount of material to a short statement
3. extraordinarily busy, overloaded with work, deeply involved
4. in addition to, beyond the ordinary, extra
5. to organize, to make preparations, to get ready for, to put in order, to plan, to arrange for
6. to depend on, to rely upon

99

The Interview ✳ 1

Tape: Part One, again — The second listening

Rewind the tape and listen to the interview again. Then answer the following questions and do the reconstruction exercise.

Detailed Questions

These detailed comprehension questions may be asked after the second listening to the interview. They do not appear in the student's book.

1. What is the self-help project that Connie is working with?
2. What are Connie's responsibilities with the project?
3. How far along is the project at this time? When will it probably be finished?
4. What do we learn about the interviewer's son?
5. What is the Farmer's Home Administration?
6. How does Connie decide which families get into the project? What does the screening process involve?
7. What difficulties do the self-help project families face?
8. Who is eligible to borrow money to be in this project?
9. What schedule has Connie been using in this project? If you were working in the project, explain how you would accumulate forty hours a week (using Connie's schedule).
10. From what you have heard, what are the difficulties in her job?
11. From what you have heard, what are the pleasures Connie gets from her job?
12. Did you learn anything about the interviewer?

Reconstruction

The exercise which is given in the student's book on page 100 should be done after the second listening to the interview.

The Dialogue ✳ 3

Tapes: Part Three — A conversation among Connie, John, and Paula

Lesson Ten, Connie Snow, building contractor, continues with the third part of the taped material. Connie is in her office. She is meeting with John and Paula, husband and wife, who are making the final decision about whether or not to get involved with the self-help housing project. She has put her phone on hold and made room on her crowded desk for a teapot and three mugs. After listening, answer the questions.

CONNIE. All right, now that you've seen the pictures and the floor plans, which of the three houses do you think you like best?

PAULA. That's an easy one.

JOHN. We're agreed on that ... you go ahead.

PAULA. Well, we figure that the two bedroom cape is going to be big enough for us.

JOHN. We figure that ....well ... um ... we figure that we probably won't have children for a while, and with the cape it will be easy to build on an extra room or two, when we need them.

PAULA. Also, the cape seems to fit in better with the houses in the neighborhood where we'd be building.

CONNIE. It sounds to me that you've pretty much decided to get into the project.

PAULA. Yeah, we really like the idea.

JOHN. Yeah, but with those reservations we talked about before.

CONNIE. Such as. . . ?

JOHN. Well, you remember ... most of all it's that thirty hours of work a week. That seems like so much time. That figures out to fifteen hours a week for each of us.

PAULA. And we both have full-time jobs.

CONNIE. Well, you remember that friends and relatives, anybody, can help too, and their time counts. Paula, didn't you say you have a good friend who could probably put in some time?

PAULA. Well, yeah, and I found out yesterday that my brother and his wife are willing to put in quite a bit of time.

JOHN. And also my father. He says he'd really like to help.

PAULA. But the other thing that we have to repeat to you is that we just don't know very much about building. Now my brother's different. He's just finished doing a rehab on his house, so he's really good. But we're, frankly, novices.

JOHN. And my father ... well, to give you an idea ... he's an English teacher.

CONNIE. English teacher? Well, there are worse things than English teachers. The truth is that I almost became an English teacher myself, so I think there's hope for him too.

JOHN. Well, if you say so. I mean, I hope you're right.

CONNIE. Look. There are some others in this new group who are in the same boat. And that's the reason why I always give the two week course in basics of building — hammering, sawing, measuring, safety on the job, all the basics. Trust me, you'll be in good shape after you have the course, and then with each new step in the project, we teach you what you need to know.

JOHN. Well, um ... you're very ... what's the word ... persuasive. You're very persuasive. And, let's face it, the bottom line is after a year of hard work, hon, we'll have our own home, and we'll have built it ourselves.

PAULA. Yeah, that's the point ... and at half the cost it would be if we didn't do the work ourselves.

CONNIE. Well, does it sound like you're ready for us.

PAULA. O.K. John?

JOHN. Well, yeah. O.K. Paula?

PAULA. O.K.

CONNIE. O.K. then. Good! Congratulations. A week from Friday the course starts. Bring a hammer and a tape measure.

PAULA. Wow. All settled. I guess we might as well sell the TV.

JOHN. No babies this year.

PAULA. That's for sure.

101

Questions

The discussion questions given in the student's book on page 101 should be used after listening to the dialogue.

The Interactive Listening ✳ 4

Tape: Part Four — Listen, visualize, and draw.

Listen to the tape. Visualize what you hear. Then following the instructions, finish the drawings given on page 101 of the student's book based on the description you hear.

1. From the immense bedroom I looked down upon the beautiful garden. It was rectangular in shape and shaded from the west by three very large oak trees. Below my windows on the north side of the garden, I enjoyed the sight of the oval swimming pool with two people splashing around in it. At its right were two small cabins where guests and family members could dress after swimming. Underneath the window I could see hundreds and hundreds of beautiful red and white roses in full bloom.

2. It was a strange street, built up on only one side because of the train tracks facing it. In the middle of the block stood a three story brick building that housed the ice and coal company and its offices. To the right of that stood a one story building that was deserted. At one time it had been occupied by a welder, but now all one could see were the W and E which remained on the shabby sign. To the left of the building there was a small auto body company with three cars ready to be fixed standing in its small front yard. On the other side of the auto body shop was the Mobil station which had been there for thirty-three years. On the other side of the now vacant welding company was an industrial bakery, which still baked bread for large institutions in the growing town. And next to the bakery only one structure remained, the one I lived in. The house, now old, had belonged to my grandfather who had founded the baking company and had lived there as had my father. "Why don't you move from that terrible neighborhood?" friends asked. How could I explain to them that the smells from the bakery and the sight of the trains passing by were things that were part of me.

Answers to the interactive listening exercise

1.

2.

The Projects

A *choice of communicative activities*

The projects are designed to be done concurrently with the listening work. The explanations for the projects start on page 105 of the student's book.

ANNOUNCER. This is the end of Lesson Ten. But wait, before you go — Ed, could you come over here a minute, please?

INTERVIEWER. Sure. What do you want?

ANNOUNCER. Well, I just had an idea. Why don't we ask the students what they've learned about you during all these interviews?

INTERVIEWER. Well, I don't know. I guess that might be interesting. Sure, why not!

ANNOUNCER. O.K. Well then, students, think back over the ten lessons and try to recall what you've learned about our interviewer. Then working with a partner or two, write out a list of what you remember which you can share with your class.

INTERVIEWER. What? You mean things like the problem I had with my refrigerator?

ANNQUNCER. Sure, and the fact that you are retired after years of . . .

INTERVIEWER. Wait, hold it. Don't give too much away. It'll be fun to find out how much the class remembers when they put their heads together.

ANNOUNCER. Right, and when they're done, that will be the end of *People at Work.*

104

TEACHER'S RESOURCE HANDBOOKS

Language Teaching Techniques. 35 basic in-class techniques with variations.

Experiential Language Teaching Techniques. 30 out-of-class activities for learning language and culture.

Cultural Awareness Teaching Techniques. 20 discussion techniques for language classes and other training and orientation programs.

Technology Assisted Teaching Techniques. 40 student-centered techniques using 14 of the most common types of equipment from brown paper and slide projectors to PC's and VCR's.

The ESL Miscellany. A cultural and linguistic inventory of American English.

Taking Students Abroad. A complete guide for teachers.

From the Experiment in International Living — **The NEWCOMERS series:**

Opening Lines. A 1-volume 30-lesson curriculum—4 ability levels—for ESL and literacy skills.

Shifting Gears 1 & 2. A 2-volume curriculum of 48 lessons for learning workplace skills and behavior and ESL.

Settling In 1 & 2. A 2-volume curriculum of 65 lessons for U.S. cultural orientation.

Teaching Teachers. (1) an overview of teacher training and the supervisor's role; (2) procedures and opinions on communication and feedback, training and administration, and observation and evaluation; (3) case studies of cross-cultural critical incidents; (4) plans for 20 teacher training sessions.

SUPPLEMENTARY MATERIALS HANDBOOKS

Lexicarry: An illustrated vocabulary builder for second languages. There is an English wordlist with over 3500 words keyed to the pictures given at the back of the book.

Lexicarry Posters. 25 wall charts. ◆ **54 Function Flashcards from Lexicarry.** Easy-to-handle strips illustrate situations requiring functional language.

Index Card Games for ESL ◆ **Index Card Games for French** ◆ **Index Card Games for Spanish.** The 6 card games explained in each of these handbooks are easy to prepare and play using 3x5 index cards. These are student-centered, group activities which provide practice with vocabulary, structure, spelling, questioning, and conversation. Sample games are given in the target language.

Families: 10 card games for language learners. 40 colorful playing cards are included.

Conversation Inspirations for ESL. Over 1,200 conversation topics and 6 distinctive conversation activities.

Getting A Fix on Vocabulary. Using words in the news. A vocabulary builder focused on the affix system in English, with exercises and words in the context of news articles.

Comics and Conversation. Using uncaptioned cartoons by Sergio Aragones to elicit conversation and develop vocabulary.

READERS FOR ADVANCED BEGINNERS

Begin in English. 14 comic plays, stories, folk tales, and histories with exercises.

From the Beginning. A first reader in American History with exercises.

INTERMEDIATE READERS

The following books are called vocabureaders. The readings are brief. Each one is followed by vocabulary-building exercises focused on key words highlighted in the texts. Supplementary material, suggestions for the teacher and the answers are given at the back of the books.

American Holidays. Exploring the traditions, customs, and backgrounds of our national holidays.

Summer Olympic Games. Exploring the individual athletic events in international competition.

The Zodiac. Exploring human qualities and characteristics. Excellent conversation starters.

Potluck. Exploring American foods and meals.

Money. Exploring the Ways we use it.

INTERPLAY ESL

Max in America, Book 1 ◆ Max in America, Book 2 ◆ Max in America, Teacher's Handbook ◆ Max in America, Narrative Picture Poster Cards. A basic communicative skills text for adults of all ages. Book 1 is a high-beginning text for the "false beginner." Book 2 is for low intermediates. The Teacher's Handbook provides important material not given in the texts.

The Grammar Handbook, Part 1 ◆ The Grammar Handbook, Part 2. The books, designed for in-class use, provide a simple grammar explanation, a work sheet for use with in-class activities, and a choice of several techniques for teaching the grammar points of the lesson. Part 1 is for "false beginners" and Part 2 for intermediate students.

Grammar Exercises, Part 1 ◆ Grammar Exercises, Part 2. These two books cover the same grammar as The Grammar Handbooks, but they are designed for out-of-class use, for homework or self-study, for use with or without the Handbooks. All the exercises are contextualized for high-interest and motivation, and the answers are provided at the back of the book.

Smalltown Daily. A multilevel reader (elementary, intermediate and advanced) based on 288 authentic newspaper articles. 6 teaching techniques are suggested. A topical index sorts out 25 fields of interest.

OTHER LISTENING MATERIALS

Stranger in Town. A "radio play" for building listening and reading skills and cultural awareness. Student script/text and tape.

Biographical Sketches for Listening. 20 winners of the Nobel Prize are descibed in listening passages. Workbook includes prelistening and cloz exercises.

For further information or to order, please write to **Pro Lingua Associates, 15 Elm St., Brattleboro, Vermont 05301,** *or call us at* 802-257-7779
We accept VISA and MASTERCARD orders by phone.